The Executive Protection
Professional's Manual

The Executive Protection Professional's Manual

Philip Holder
Donna Lea Hawley

Butterworth–Heinemann
An Imprint of Elsevier
Boston Oxford Johannesburg Melbourne New Delhi Singapore

Butterworth–Heinemann is an imprint of Elsevier

Copyright © 1998 by Butterworth–Heinemann

 A member of the Reed Elsevier group

∞ Recognizing the importance of preserving what has been written, Elsevier prints its books on acid-free paper whenever possible.

 Elsevier supports the efforts of American Forests and the Global ReLeaf program in its campaign for the betterment of trees, forests, and our environment.

Library of Congress Cataloging-in-Publication Data

Holder, Philip, 1951–
  The executive protection professional's manual / Philip Holder, Donna Lea Hawley.
    p.   cm.
  Includes index.
  ISBN-13: 978-0-7506-9868-9   ISBN-10: 0-7506-9868-3
    1. Executives—Protection—Handbooks, manuals, etc.   2. Terrorism—Prevention—Handbooks, manuals, etc.   3. Industries—Security measures—Handbooks, manuals, etc.   I. Hawley, Donna Lea, 1946–   .   II. Title.
  HV8290.H65   1997
  363.28'9—dc21
                                                                        97–16800
                                                                        CIP

British Library Cataloguing-in-Publication Data
A catalogue record for this book is available from the British Library.

The publisher offers special discounts on bulk orders of this book.
For information, please contact:

Manager of Special Sales
Elsevier
200 Wheeler Road, 6th Floor
Burlington, MA 01803
Tel: 781-313-4700
Fax: 781-313-4882

For information on all our security publications,
contact our World Wide Web home page at: http://www.bh.com

10 9 8 7 6 5

Printed in the United States of America

Recently I was visiting a community where some of my past principals lived. I ran into an old friend (a mutual friend of one of these principals) and was saddened to hear that one individual to whom I had provided protective services years ago had been murdered since my move from that area. He had apparently decided that he no longer required an executive protection professional (EPP). I had not seen this person for many years, so I have no idea what prompted the decision to cease the use of an EPP, but apparently it was a fatal one.

The EPP works behind the scenes and usually gets little or no recognition for the valuable service that he or she provides. The EPP is often the last line of defense between his or her principal and the serious injury or death of that person. Having lived this experience firsthand, I would like to dedicate this book to the many unsung heroes who silently protect the life and limb of others, often at great personal risk.

—Philip Holder

Contents

Preface

Turn on the news or pick up a newspaper on any given day, and you will see evidence of the rise in terrorism, abductions, murders, and burglaries. Bombings have killed innocent civilians as well as law enforcement personnel, politicians, and military personnel. Sports figures, businesspeople, news reporters, and entertainment personalities have increasingly become the targets of radicals, fanatics, and psychopaths. With the increase in violence and the lack of respect some individuals and groups in our society have for others, it is no surprise that people are seeking protection. Over the next decade the demand for executive protection professionals is certain to rise. This book is intended to give you a greater insight into what you will need to know and what will be expected of you as an executive protection professional (EPP).

This book is intended to help those with an interest in the executive protection field better understand what is involved in being an EPP. It is not intended or implied that after reading this book you are qualified to begin work as an EPP. It is intended to give you greater insight into the field and to help prepare you by expanding your knowledge in the field of executive protection. The information given in this book is for reference only. The authors and publisher do not in any way endorse or condone any illegal activity or act. The authors and publisher do not recommend or encourage anyone to take any action or perform any skill set out in this book, and disclaim any and all liability and assume no responsibility for the use or misuse of the information in this book.

1

The Executive Protection Professional's Job

Executive protection is an exciting and rewarding career. It is also a very specialized line of work requiring diligent, comprehensive, and diverse areas of study. The executive protection person is a highly trained professional. He or she must be well equipped to handle the immense responsibility entrusted to him or her. He or she carries the responsibility of providing for the protection, health, welfare, and possibly the life of another human being. A competent executive protection professional (EPP) never takes this role lightly.

Let's first dispel some myths. The biggest, toughest, grizzliest person in town will not necessarily make the best EPP. Neither will the guy who thinks that because he has a black belt in martial arts, he is eminently qualified to be an EPP. It is certainly important to have effective and competent defensive-tactics skills in order to deal with an aggressor should the need arise. Frankly, though, if a threat escalates to the point where you, as an EPP, must put your hands on someone, you have, in most cases, failed at some other point in the execution of your duties. The EPP is not present to throw out undesirables or to bully unwanted guests. Likewise, the true professional does not view his or her role as one of a soldier who should engage the enemy. To the contrary, the professional knows that he or she should disengage the enemy and get the principal to safety as quickly as possible. As well, the professional is not hired to simply stand around waiting for possible trouble. He or she has many other important duties.

The EPP has many duties that you must always keep in mind. As an EPP, you are responsible not only for protecting your principal from those who would do intentional harm but also for protecting your principal from accidental harm and from embarrassment. Let's say that your principal is going to make a speech at a large convention. It would certainly be embarrassing and a potentially dangerous situation if he or she were to walk onto the stage to speak, trip over a microphone cord, and fall into the orchestra pit. An EPP is always looking for dangers as seemingly small as that microphone cord, stretched across the stage. When you see a potential danger, you should offer a warning to the principal such as "Sir/madam, please watch that microphone cord on your way to the podium."

An effective EPP is one who has learned to keep a low profile for both himself or herself and the principal. The less attention you draw to your principal, the more you reduce the chance of threat. Likewise, the less attention you draw to yourself (the EPP should be undetectable and not be perceived as a bodyguard by onlookers), and the less you are distracted by others, the safer your principal will be from attack and from prying media reporters, curiosity seekers, or fans. This of course becomes a more complicated issue when you are working in celebrity protection. Celebrities often have a promotional need to be in the limelight. Their fans expect to see them, and this high profile helps in spreading their name and reputation. At the same time that it is promoting the principal's career, it makes your job much more complicated. In this situation you no longer have the advantage of moving your principal out of the view of prying eyes, and his or her exposure to harm increases.

The EPP understands the concept of conflict avoidance. As an EPP, you are more than a source of protection. You, in effect, become an ambassador or public-relations representative for your principal. Your actions will directly affect how people perceive your principal. Remember the old sayings "You are known by the company you keep" and "Guilt through association." You must ask, What image does my principal strive to create? Your demeanor can help your principal accomplish a goal, or, if you behave poorly, your behavior can destroy his or her image. If you are destructive to the image your principal is attempting to create, you will find yourself "between assignments" (unemployed) most of your career. You must always strive to have your principal viewed in a positive light. If you are a bully, a braggart, a showoff, or a hothead, it will reflect negatively on your principal.

There are additional responsibilities and duties that are often overlooked by those wishing to enter this profession. First, an EPP must know the principal. You must be fully aware of what his or her purpose in hiring you is. You must know how he or she views you. Sometimes, primarily in corporate executive protection, the EPP is viewed by the executive/principal as a necessary inconvenience that he or she must accept along with his or her position. Some entertainers may want a bodyguard as a showpiece. Other principals will view you as a vital part of their staff. You can do your job more effectively if you know your principal's goals, habits, and routine (although "routine" should be politely discouraged). Second, you must be skilled in the proper routing of luggage, advance reconnaissance, intelligence gathering, crowd control, motorcade procedures, legal requirements and limitations, proper, safe, and legal use of firearms, defensive tactics, legal and appropriate use of force, package and mail inspection, building and auto search (for eavesdropping, tracking devices, explosives, and so on), threat analysis, arranging transportation (by air, land, rail, or other means), educating your principal, and route planning. Third, you must have the skills for meticulous planning, effective use of resources, effective assignment of responsibility (when you are working with a team), and proper management, control, and confidentiality of information.

As an executive protection agent, you must provide for (1) the security and (2) the comfort of your principal. At the same time, you must create as little intrusion into your principal's lifestyle as possible. This is no easy feat. You must be sure that if you are on a trip with your principal, your principal's luggage (as well as his or her family's or friend's luggage) goes to the proper room(s) in a timely fashion. You will often be responsible for arranging both air and ground transportation. You must be sure that you acquire flights, rental cars, and other facilities that will be pleasing to your principal.

When possible (this is much easier when you are working with a team), you should "advance" the destination. This simply means to go ahead of time and check the lay of the land, inspect the room(s), know the exits, and the like. As well, you may need to do some intelligence gathering. For instance, does your principal have any enemies in the area in which he or she plans to travel? Are there any parades or events that might create a traffic or transportation problem? What is the forecast for the weather? You may need to make sure that there are umbrellas on hand or recommend to your principal that a raincoat be brought along. Is there any construction on roads in the area? Have you planned both a route and two alternate routes in case of a problem? (These seemingly small things will increase your worth in your principal's eyes.) If there is more than one car in the entourage, are the drivers skilled in defensive maneuvering procedures?

The EPP must have at least a basic knowledge of the law pertaining to the use of force or firearms and to any other restrictions or requirements (which may differ from area to area) within the context of his or her job description. It will not look good for you or your principal if one or both of you end up in jail because of some silly oversight on your part.

When planning, the EPP must do a threat analysis in order to determine the degree of precaution and security that will be necessary. This is important because the degree of protection will to a large degree impact on the degree of intrusion that will exist into your principal's daily life. You must determine what the degree of threat is and coordinate your resources accordingly. Never assume that there is no threat. There is a saying among executive protection professionals, "Today is the day that it will happen." If you, as an EPP, tell yourself this each morning, you will be less likely to let your guard down at the wrong time.

An important characteristic of an EPP is confidentiality. Anything that you see or hear on the job must go no further, even to the extent of something seemingly trivial. What is trivial to one person may not seem trivial to another. Even your client's name should not be given to those who have no need (in the principal's interest) to know. Talk to no one about your principal, his or her family, friends, or affairs. A wise EPP won't even talk to the principal's family members about his or her principal or vice versa. It isn't your job to play Paul Revere. Keep your comments to yourself, or you may be perceived by your principal and his family as a gossip. If this happens, you will lose everyone's trust and confidence. You will earn a great deal of respect by following this one simple rule: Keep your mouth shut.

SPECIALTY AREAS

There are different specialties in the profession of executive protection. You may chose corporate executive protection, celebrity protection, or possibly dignitary protection. Although there are some differences that make each unique, in general, the major guidelines that the EPP needs to follow are fundamentally the same. Also, there is the choice between working as a single agent or on a team. Both have advantages and disadvantages, but again, the fundamentals of the job are the same in all specialty areas.

THE EXECUTIVE PROTECTION PROFESSIONAL'S ROLE

As we indicated before, as an EPP, it is your job to make sure that your principal feels secure and comfortable. In great part this is either going to happen or not happen based on the principal's faith in your character and abilities. This cannot be stressed enough. You must shield him or her from intended and accidental harm, provide for his or her comfort, organize and prepare, be close by and yet not too close, represent your principal in a dignified and professional manner, always be aware, maintain a low profile, make yourself knowledgeable about laws and restrictions, and prevent embarrassment to your principal. In short, your job is to do whatever is necessary to accomplish and assure all of these goals.

The words "That's not my job" should never be thought or spoken. That phrase and/or attitude could spell the beginning of the end of your career as an EPP. This does not imply that you should take on the role of a servant; however, you must accept that you, as an EPP, will have many diverse duties. Short of taking on tasks that would detract from your main function as a protector, you should not consider yourself above accepting other duties that may enhance the bond between you and your principal. If you are asked to do something that would reduce your effectiveness as an EPP, there are polite and diplomatic ways to tell your principal that it would not be appropriate or in the principal's best interest for you to do the particular task that he or she has asked you to do. You might say, "I would be happy to do that for you under different circumstances, but right now, your safety is my primary concern. If you don't mind, I'll have someone else handle that for you. I'll follow up to be sure it gets done." In this way you would be showing that you are interested in the principal's needs and do not feel that you are above certain tasks while at the same time showing that you are focused on your primary function as his or her protector.

The job of an executive protection agent is a sacred trust. It is a great honor to have someone place enough trust in you to put his or her life into your hands. You need always to be aware of and value this trust. You must honor this trust by conducting yourself in an honest and professional manner. In order to do this, you must know your profession inside and out. One mistake could mean the life of another.

2

Attributes of a Good Executive Protection Professional

All good executive protection professionals (Epps) generally possess similar attributes. While some of the attributes may be inherent within some people, most of them can be developed or enhanced by those who want to enter and excel in the profession.

APPEARANCE

Your appearance is important, but some aspects of it will depend on the type of principal you have. While high-profile entertainers may like huge bodybuilder types, most clients want someone who will fit into their party and not stand out as a bodyguard. This means that almost anyone can satisfy the appearance requirements as far as physical type goes. However, you should be of average weight, not too skinny and not so overweight that you can't perform all the physical demands of the job. You shouldn't have any visible tattoos. Your haircut should be similar to that of the person you will be protecting. If your principal has a tan, so should you; likewise for a lack of suntan. Keep your jewelry to a watch and possibly one ring, but nothing that is flashy or will call attention to you. If your principal dresses formally or casually, you need to dress formally or casually for the occasion.

Your appearance also includes the way you walk, stand, and move in general. Learn to fit in with those you are protecting. They may be conservative in movement, gesture as they talk, walk fast or slow, or play sports. You should be able to move with them undetected while you perform your duties. Your appearance should make you fit into the picture so you look like you belong and not so that you will stand out in any way and be noticed.

DEMEANOR

Your demeanor is a delicate balance. On the one hand, you are the employee of a person who is probably more powerful and wealthy than you and who is your boss; on the other hand, you are the professional who is responsible for your employer's safety and well-being. You must develop respect for and receive respect from your employer.

5

While you may never be "equals," you should never act in a subservient way that will be noticed by others who will then identify you in your role and perhaps make you a target. This is something you will need to discuss clearly with your principal so that he or she doesn't misinterpret your demeanor as disrespect. Don't try to be friends or get personally involved with your principal or his or her family.

To best serve your principal, you should always be polite to everyone you meet. This will reflect well on your principal and will also allow you to get the greatest cooperation from others. You should speak well and clearly. You should use good manners. Even when you are verbally or physically preventing someone from gaining access to your principal, you should be polite and mannerly. You must always conduct yourself as a professional.

PHYSICAL SKILLS

You will need a variety of physical skills ranging from self-defense to formal table manners. General health is an often ignored element of physical skill. If you get sick with anything from the flu to a heart attack, you won't be able to protect your principal. Take preventive measures such as shots to stave off those illnesses you can prevent, eat a healthful diet to avoid potential long-term conditions, and get annual medical checkups to screen yourself for potential problems. Dress for the weather so you don't suffer from heat exhaustion, cold, exposure, or rain. Whenever possible, get as much sleep as you can.

It goes without saying that you should be in the best physical condition you can attain. Schedule exercise time for when you are off as well as during days you are on duty. Develop strength, endurance, and flexibility so you can perform at your best in every situation. You never know when you will have to spend hours sitting in a car and stay alert and physically ready, stand or walk for long periods without cramping or fatigue, and go with irregular sleep or meals for periods of time. Depending on where you live, you can set up your own home gymnasium or join a local facility that offers you the best variety of equipment and the longest hours (since your hours may be irregular). Try to exercise daily. If you are traveling, many hotels offer exercise facilities. If your principal works out, you can exercise at the same time. Otherwise, make sure another detail member is on duty while you go to the gym.

MENTAL SKILLS

You must have confidence in yourself. You must know that you have received the best training possible, that you are in the best physical condition possible, that you know every aspect of your job, that you have done everything possible to ensure the safety of your principal, and that you are able to handle any potential problem or attack. You must be mentally able to continue to learn, and you must want to learn new ways and techniques. You will need to adapt to the ways of life of your principal, and you cannot judge any behavior or attribute of your principal. Once you accept the assignment, your only purpose is to protect your principal. His or her personal idiosyncrasies are not yours to judge.

You must be able to keep your mind on the job at hand and not let your mind wander to personal problems, an attractive passerby, the football score on the radio, or anything else not directly related to your job of protecting your principal. You must be able to control your emotions. You cannot let anger block your judgment. You cannot let your own personal life, either joy or hurt, enter your professional mind. You cannot joke and laugh to the extent that it takes your mind away from your job. You must be able to control fear or rage so you can perform your job in a crisis. Above all, leave your ego at home.

YOUR SUPPORT NETWORK

Help often comes from the most unlikely places. Many times it filters upward instead of downward. Aside from it being the right thing to do, and better for both your principal's and your own image, there are practical reasons for being a nice person. If you are viewed as arrogant, uncooperative, and basically obnoxious, others will have no incentive to help or cooperate with you. Being snotty to the headwaiter (even to speed up your principal's dinner) will probably just get your coffee spat in and slow up your next room-service call. If you treat all those whom you encounter, from the trash collector to the president of the United States, with kindness and respect, you will earn the respect and cooperation of others. A bully's respect only lasts until he or she turns his or her back.

It is often the people at the grass-roots level who can offer the greatest help. The doorman at a hotel can tip you off if you have asked him to look out for a particular person or vehicle. (Don't forget to tip him, too, and be generous.) The maid may permit you discreet access to areas that otherwise you may not have access to, or that you would have to go through time-consuming channels to gain access to. Be appreciative; these are the frontline people who can be of invaluable assistance. Don't talk down to them or put yourself above them. You all put on your pants the same way.

OTHER EXECUTIVE PROTECTION PROFESSIONALS

There will be times when you will be working alongside of other EPPs employed by principals other than your own. This may be at a business meeting, a banquet, or any type of social event. Create a rapport with these fellow agents. Don't compete with them. You will all make out better by working together. If your principal does business frequently with the same people, you will become acquainted with their EPPs and learn which ones are reliable and which are not. You will learn which ones are trustworthy and which ones may not be. Up to the point where it might compromise your principal's safety or security, work with these people. You may exchange general information such as building plans and parking-lot diagrams that you have gotten from the building maintenance supervisor, local contacts for auto repair and other services, advance reconnaissance information, and so on. Expect them to reciprocate. Remember, this is general information only. This can be defined as information that they could easily obtain on their own, but that you have already acquired and will share to save them some legwork.

3

Types of Principals

People needing personal protection come from many diverse professions and backgrounds. Professional people who never before felt the need for protection are now facing dangers rarely encountered in the past. Business executives, doctors and other medical professionals, sports figures, politicians, entertainers, and social, political, or religious spokespeople are among those who often require protection. For our purposes, we can divide prospective principals into four categories. These categories are business, entertainment, political, and social.

Principals within the business classification include chief executive officers (CEOs) of profitable companies, negotiators, high-profile attorneys, couriers of valuable commodities or information, corporate research and development personnel, and other people who are privy to secret information. Entertainment principals include movie and television personalities, sports figures, recording stars, and fashion models. Political principals include politicians, spokespeople for environmental groups, lobbyists, civil rights activists, and religious leaders. People who require an EPP for social reasons include famous or wealthy people and their spouses and children.

Although these four classifications have some commonalities, they all have unique differences and specialized needs as well. When choosing executive protection as a career, you will need to decide which type of principal is most attractive to your career goals. Whether you prefer to work as a single agent or as part of a security detail (an EPP team or squad) will also be affected by the type of principal(s) you choose to work for. With large corporate business principals, for instance, you are more likely to work as part of a detail of security professionals. With a sports figure or moderately known entertainer, you will probably work as a single agent.

BUSINESS PRINCIPALS

The business principal is usually a relatively low-profile client. This will make your job easier in certain respects. Your job often will revolve around transporting your principal (and/or his or her family) to meetings, events, luncheons, and the like. This is often a job of "hurry up and wait."

Principals in this group will often view you as a necessary evil and inconvenience that they must accept as part of the position. You can expect to work long hours with little personal thanks or gratitude (except for the money and often fringe benefits). This is fine for some people. If you prefer a team working environment, a security detail may be for you, and working for a business principal is where you will most often find it. This provides you with the flexibility to advance locations (often not an option for a single EPP) and with the added benefit of sharing the responsibilities with others on your detail.

Some of the dangers that principals in the business classification face are kidnapping, robbery, attack by a disgruntled employee, or retaliation by a beaten business competitor. Depending on their business (if they do animal testing, make dangerous or toxic chemicals, or work in the nuclear energy industry, for example), they may have a multitude of fanatical enemies with whom they have absolutely no personal connection. They are also targeted, on occasion, by individuals looking to make money through contrived and unfounded lawsuits.

Let's say that your principal is the CEO of a large chemical company that produces a toxic substance. Someone from a fringe environmental group could perceive your principal as responsible for the world's ills and attempt to assassinate your principal as an example of what might happen to others in that field if they continue to "destroy the earth." These terrorist tactics are hard to predict because of the lack of any personal contact between your principal and the attacker. Someone after money might bump into your principal and then fall to the ground claiming injury because your principal pushed him or her. Don't assume that anything is too bizarre for some people to attempt.

ENTERTAINMENT PRINCIPALS

The entertainment field, by its nature, is a high-profile industry. This in itself creates unique problems for the EPP. You, by the nature of your profession as an EPP, attempt to keep the lowest possible profile. Your entertainment principal, by the nature of his or her profession, often needs to keep a high profile. This makes your job doubly difficult because you must protect your principal and at the same time conduct yourself in a way that shows your principal in a positive light with his or her public. The saying "You are known by the company you keep" is very true in executive protection. An unprofessional "bodyguard" (as opposed to a professional EPP) can cause an otherwise respected entertainer to be looked at as an unfriendly and obnoxious spoiled star. The bad press that an unprofessional or poorly trained EPP can generate (in a skirmish with a fan, autograph seeker, or photographer) can occur in a split second. It may then take thousands of dollars and months or even years of hard public-relations work to repair the damage created in that brief moment. The dangers present to the entertainment principal include kidnapping, assault by an obsessed fan, accidental injury from overzealous fans, interference in the course of normal daily activity by fans and admirers, and threats from former lovers or business partners or from unscrupulous individuals looking for the opportunity to sue over any number of contrived circumstances ranging from assault to palimony.

POLITICAL PRINCIPALS

Political principals primarily face danger from fanatics and activists who differ in philosophical view from their own. The EPP's job becomes doubly difficult if the principal himself or herself is fanatical in his or her views. Nevertheless, once you accept the job, it is your obligation to protect and care for the safety and comfort of your principal. Within the political classification of principal, you are often dealing with emotionally charged issues. It is a much more volatile climate to work in. An intruder will often be fanatical and irrational and have no regard for the consequences of his or her actions for himself or herself or the consequences to others. Often the intruder's goal is to make a big scene in order to attract the press and bring as much attention to his or her views as possible.

Threats in the political area of executive protection may include attempts to spit on and/or insult and demean your principal in other ways, throwing of paint or blood, attacks with guns, knives, or clubs, and bombs and/or other terrorist actions. The perpetrator may plan an attack in advance, or it may be the result of a spontaneous emotional outburst. This category usually houses the most unpredictable intruders. Their desires are fueled by emotion rather than common sense.

SOCIAL PRINCIPALS

The main threat against social principals is kidnapping. This threat will most often come from an unknown source. Kidnapping is usually a well-planned and organized attack. It is difficult to predict this type of attack unless prior threats have been made. As a professional EPP, you must protect your principal from this threat without appearing paranoid to your principal or causing your principal and his or her family to be fearful.

BEING PREPARED

In order to respond effectively to any of the aforementioned intruders, you must be properly trained and must properly train your principal. Of course, it would not be very tactful to tell your principal that you plan to train him or her, but that is exactly what you must subtly do. Your principal must know the "game plan" for any given possibility. You might consider approaching your principal in this way: "Excuse me, sir (or ma'am), at your earliest convenience, could I speak with you briefly? I would like to get some information from you for my employer profile. The information will help me to better serve you with the smallest amount of intrusion into your daily routine." Then get your principal to commit to a specific time.

The following are some questions that you might ask when you have your EPP/principal interview. All knowledge gathered about your principal will help you better prepare for his or her well-being.

1. Ask for the names of all immediate family members, their contact numbers, addresses, and other relevant information.
2. Ask for information about extended family members living outside the principal's primary residence (parents, grandparents, aunts, uncles, and so on).

3. Assure confidentiality and ask about mistresses, love interests, and so on. This becomes even more significant if the principal is married.
4. Find out which car the principal normally rides in.
5. Ask to what clubs and associations the principal belongs.
6. Ask for a list of enemies, possible enemies, business competitors, and key employees.
7. Find out about any medical problems or medications that the principal takes. This includes food or drug allergies.
8. Ask about housekeeping (both at home and business locations), laundry, auto repair, and other maintenance people. In other words, find out all you can about peripheral activities.
9. Ask if the principal has or carries a firearm.
10. Find out if the principal uses alcohol or other drugs.
11. Ask about any fetishes the principal may have. Again, assure confidentiality.
12. Find out the principal's recreational activities and other interests (sports, hobbies, and so on).

Learn as much as you can about your principal. Try to "get into his or her head." Get a feel for how your principal thinks and reacts. Analyze to the best of your ability and training what type of person he or she is under the veneer that he or she may show. A thorough understanding of the person will give you a better idea of how he or she will behave in different situations.

When interviewing your principal, watch the little things he or she says and does. You will find out just as much, if not more, about your principal by the seemingly inconsequential things he or she does. Things that to many would seem insignificant are in fact excellent indicators about personality traits. Learn to read between the lines. In part, you must be an amateur psychologist. This should be practiced not only in your interview of your principal, but each and every day as well.

Next, you will want to set up a time to review daily procedures. You might continue the conversation by saying, "Also, sir (ma'am), I would like to set aside a time when we can go over both day-to-day safety procedures and emergency procedures. I want to keep you informed about procedures so that you will feel confident and secure about what you will do, and what you can expect me to do, in both nuisance and threat situations. What time would be best for you? This will take about an hour. It might be useful to you to review that information on occasion. We can set up those times on the basis of need and at your convenience, of course." Once you have established a time for the day-to-day and emergency procedures, you are ready to start training your principal. He or she must know exactly what you expect him or her to do, and what you will be doing, in both casual and emergency situations. This will make the interaction between the two of you efficient and effective.

It is a good idea to practice or rehearse with your principal. When it is convenient for your principal, plan a trip. It might be from one building on his or her property to another. Tell your principal to imagine that you are traveling from a business meeting to his or her favorite restaurant. Rehearse how you will organize the principal's departure, transit, arrival, entry, and seating. Rehearse your respective seating positions and your relative positions when walking together. Have your principal imagine (or use another person to simulate) a passerby walking from various different approaches toward you and your principal. This will give the principal an opportunity to see how you shift positions and how he or she will need to cooperate in realigning his or her position. Rehearsing this and other scenarios can be a valuable tool in developing a working relationship with your principal.

From something as simple as his or her walking on your protective side to what to do under gunfire, you should prearrange the general procedures that you will both take in an emergency. Think of all the possibly dangerous situations that the nonprofessional would probably overlook and then form a plan to address them. The few minutes that it takes to instruct your principal on where to walk, sit, or stand and what to do in an emergency could very well save his or her life. The most important factor is to keep it simple. Complicated plans will be forgotten in an emergency.

Here is an example. Assume that you are working as a sole agent. In day-to-day circumstances, you know that it is important for your principal to know about relative positioning. This refers to your principal's position relative to you and to the immediate surroundings. Since you should always be on your principal's most open or vulnerable side, you might offer this instruction: "Sir (or ma'am), remember that you should be positioned so that I am in your central vision when you look toward your most exposed side. If someone approaches, we will always attempt to maintain a position where I am between you and the other person. You may need to shift position on occasion to help facilitate this positioning." Make your principal aware that although you are primarily responsible for creating this formation, his or her awareness and cooperation will help things run more smoothly and provide for his or her greater safety. Reassure him that his or her safety and comfort (in that order) are your primary concern. This also lets your principal know what you will be doing so that he or she doesn't think that you are nuts when you repeatedly shift from one side to the other during the course of the day.

4

General Principles and Procedures

There are some general principles and procedures that we will classify under "miscellaneous" and will cover in this chapter. These are items that fall either into many or none of the more specific individual chapter topics. These topics are about day-to-day practices and tips that will help to make you more efficient at your job.

PHONE NUMBERS

You (and other personnel vital to your assignment and with a need to know) should always carry necessary phone numbers. These numbers should include cell phone numbers, home numbers, and work numbers with the proper phone extension, if applicable. Your list should include phone numbers of the following:

1. Other security detail members
2. Your principal's family
3. Important business contacts of your principal
4. Area hospitals
5. Poison control center
6. AAA or other motor clubs
7. Local and state police

Also, as part of your phone-number intelligence gathering, be sure to check and see if the local calling area where you will be has 911 capabilities.

REDIRECTING THE ATTACK

If you are working as part of a security detail (as opposed to working as a single agent), have a plan for any possible location and situation to redirect an attack. Your primary function is to keep your principal safe. If an attack should occur, you can reduce the risk to your principal by drawing fire away from him or her. An intruder will often use distraction as a ploy to make you lose your focus and leave your principal unguarded and vulnerable. There is no reason why you cannot and should not use that same tactic. If you can turn the intruder's attention away from your principal, you reduce the threat to your principal. This can work just as well for you as for the intruder.

As an example, let's say that you are walking down the hall of an office building with your principal. Suddenly a man jumps out from a doorway and begins to yell obscenities at your principal. Then he begins to break windows and overturns the water cooler. If you try to stop him, or even if you are overly distracted by him, it is quite possible that an accomplice may attack your principal while you are occupied with the first intruder. You can often use the same tactic successfully. Let's say an intruder approaches your principal shouting, "I'll get you for marketing that toxic widget." If you are out of arm's reach (which, incidentally, you should not be without good reason), you might yell to the intruder, "Hey, I'm the one you want. I designed that widget. I love that widget." This could very well turn the intruder's attention to you. This distraction would give you the window of opportunity you need to protect your principal.

WATCH/INVESTIGATE THE FOLLOWING PEOPLE

It is often easier for people in certain jobs to gain unauthorized access to offices and rooms where others might be questioned. These are usually "invisible" positions or jobs that we normally don't look at. Intruders will often pose in one of these positions to avoid detection. You should be aware of some commonly used subterfuges.

Spies can masquerade as secretaries or other privileged employees. Often those wishing to bring harm to your principal will plan far in advance by having operatives apply for jobs within your principal's organization. They will bide their time, earning the trust of those around them (including your principal and yourself) until they are in a position to accomplish their goal, whether it be espionage, piracy, or physical harm.

Discreetly investigate those who have access to your principal through personal relationships. A girlfriend or boyfriend may be genuine, or he or she may have infiltrated as a spy. As with privileged employees, some individuals may attempt to develop a personal relationship with your principal in order to gain access to him or her.

Intruders may disguise themselves as cleaning men or women. Common in office buildings, such workers often go unnoticed. Delivery people, repair people, and salespeople are all common in the workplace and the home and also often go unnoticed. Uniforms for workers in these professions are easy to get. The intruder may simply put on a uniform and push a cleaning cart or carry a clipboard in order to blend into the office scenery and enter without suspicion.

All such people can do physical harm to your principal, plant bugs or bombs, take photos, make photocopies of sensitive documents, and steal classified documents and other items. Assume that anything is possible, no matter how innocent or seemingly trustworthy a person may seem. Good spies will always seem innocent and trustworthy. It is their job to gain the confidence of those they seek to infiltrate or harm. The general perception is that men fill these roles. For this reason, women are particularly effective in gaining entry. A competent EPP views people in a gender-neutral fashion. Don't fall for someone's personality plus, or for a pretty smile.

SUSPECT A BOMB?

If you suspect a bomb, you must act quickly to prevent a possible disaster. You must first evacuate your principal from the area. If you are working alone, you will need to find a safe room for your principal. Either solicit the help of other security or building personnel, or find a place where your principal can lock himself or herself in from the inside of the room. Make sure that your principal's safe room is a safe distance from the suspected explosive device.

If you are working as part of a detail, all detail members should surround and evacuate the principal. You should keep the principal bent down so that all areas of his or her head and body are well shielded by the bodies of the detail members. If there are enough detail members, one may be designated to attend to contacting support personnel while the others evacuate the principal. When you are working with a detail, there is no reason for the principal to be left alone. The detail should get the principal as far away as possible. Keep in mind that this could very well be an intruder's way of forcing you to move your principal out and into the open. Evacuate the principal with great caution. If you have planned properly, you will have a procedure in place for just such an eventuality. Once you are sure of your principal's safety, the following are the next steps to take:

1. Notify your security detail's control center and have it notify the authorities (police, bomb squad). Hopefully, the bomb squad will get there quickly, and your responsibility there will be over. You should then rejoin your principal and the other detail members. If the bomb squad cannot get there quickly, or if there is imminent danger to other people, you may choose to go on to the next steps.
2. Without disturbing the device, cover the bomb with a mattress if one is available. If not, find a similar heavy object that will absorb some of the impact of an explosion.
3. Clear the area back at least 300 feet.
4. Open windows and doors.
5. Evacuate the area.
6. Allow no reentry into the area.
7. Leave defusing or moving a suspected explosive device to a professional law-enforcement bomb squad.

SAMPLE PRINCIPAL QUESTIONNAIRE

After you are hired, it is important that you have some intelligence information about your principal and about others close to your principal whom you may be called on to protect or care for. This is a sample of some of the questions that you should include. To obtain this information, an informal, verbal interview while you take notes is fine.

Principal Data
1. Enemy list or threat factors.
2. Organizations or affiliations.

3. Health needs and problems.
4. Lifestyle (social, personal, recreational). Does principal drink or take medication that might impair judgment?
5. Prejudices, moral beliefs, and the like.
6. Peculiarities, such as excessive compulsive disorders, sexual peculiarities, offbeat pastimes, or eccentricities.
7. What cover (if any) does the principal want you to use? Not all principals want to make it obvious that they have an EPP. Some may prefer to introduce you as a business associate, a personal trainer, a secretary, or something else other than an EPP.
8. List of family members' names, addresses, and phone numbers. This includes spouse, girlfriend(s)/boyfriend(s), children, mistress, and so forth.
9. Children's school and spouse's place of employment or favorite organizations, clubs, or hangouts.
10. Are there any weapons at home, in the office, or in any vehicle? You don't want an intruder to get possession of a weapon that you were unaware of. Also, you don't want your principal to accidentally shoot you in a panic situation.
11. Who handles vehicle maintenance, and where and how often is maintenance done?
12. Principal's doctor and closest medical facility.

These are some of the questions that will help you to build a practical principal profile. This is also a good time to cover some basic safety concepts with your principal. You may wish to set up code signals or words. In this way, for instance, if your principal is being detained in a conversation that he or she would like to end, your principal can subtly signal you by something as simple as adjusting his tie or her brooch. This is your cue to create an excuse that will allow him or her to end the conversation. You might intervene by saying, "Excuse me, sir/madam, you have a phone call" or something else that will allow your principal to politely be excused. Likewise, you may want to signal your principal to move behind you or that something has occurred making it necessary to leave. Two taps on your lapel might be your prearranged signal that it is time to exercise caution and leave the current location. If your principal has expressed that he or she wants you to perform other duties that might distract you from your function as an EPP, this is a good time to discuss the hazards of duties that might keep you from your primary function.

5

Legal Issues for Executive Protection Professionals

It is essential that an EPP understand the law and follow the law at all times. If you are arrested for committing a crime or a firearms violation, you won't be able to protect your principal and may cause embarrassment or disruption to your principal. If you become liable for a civil matter, you may involve your principal in a civil lawsuit for damages brought by someone you have injured. As a minimum, you should have an understanding of your legal relationship with your principal, the licensing laws of your state and the places to which you will travel with your principal, and liability for injuries you may inflict or acts you may perform on behalf of your principal. This chapter will provide only a brief outline of each of these areas. As an EPP, you must read and take courses to find out the exact nature of the law where you live and work.

LEGAL RELATIONSHIP WITH YOUR PRINCIPAL

The relationship between an EPP and a principal comes about through a contract of employment or for services. It may be in writing and contain exact details of all the elements of the contract, or it may be a verbal agreement with only generally discussed terms. This contract or agreement creates a relationship that the law calls "agency." Agency law creates duties and liabilities on both the employer, who is called the principal, and the employee, who is called the agent. The basic element of agency is that the acts of the agent are the acts of the principal. The agent can sign contracts and legally obligate the principal to the terms of the contract, and the agent can commit a civil wrong and make the principal legally obligated to pay the damages to the injured person. For example, if the agent EPP hires people and rents equipment for a motorcade, the principal is liable for payment for this. Likewise, if the agent is driving a vehicle owned or leased by the principal and negligently injures someone in an accident, the principal will be liable to pay the damages.

There is a limitation on this liability, however. To bind the principal, the agent must be acting "within the scope of his employment," which means that the EPP must be doing something that was authorized in the original contract for employment. The employer must have agreed that the EPP should do the particular act or must have given general instructions that would include that particular act for the employer to be liable for it. It may be difficult to determine what this includes in a general verbal agreement. If it is not clear what your exact duties are from your verbal agreement, then in a lawsuit you may have to refer to what duties are common in the EPP business for an agent to perform. This may be difficult since most such relationships are confidential in nature.

There is another complication in the agency relationship that may affect EPPs. Agency is a personal relationship between two parties in which the principal employs the agent to perform a certain job. The employer defines the job to be performed and gives general instructions on how it is to be carried out, and the agent performs the job within the scope of the employment agreement. In this relationship the principal will be liable for the acts of the agent. There is another legal way to contract with someone for essentially the same services, and in this relationship the service provider is called an independent contractor. An independent contractor is someone who performs a service or job for another but who makes up his or her own mind about how to accomplish and carry out the job. For example, if you want someone to drive you to a meeting, if you hire a chauffeur, he or she will be an agent, while a taxi driver will be an independent contractor. You control the chauffeur with regard to the hours of work, what duties will be performed in addition to driving, how the car is taken care of, and even giving directions as to what streets to take or speed to drive. A taxi driver will make these decisions alone and will just pick you up when requested and drop you at your destination. If the chauffeur gets into an accident, you will be liable for the damage caused, but you will not be liable for damage caused by the taxi driver because he or she is an independent contractor and is not under your control or acting on your behalf.

Some EPPs will be independent contractors; others will be agents. You should have this distinction clearly in your mind when you start a position and should discuss it with your principal. If you work exclusively for one person and are not part of a private business such as a detective or security agency, you may be an employee, and thus an agent. If, however, you are one member of a detective or security agency, if you have other clients to whom you also offer EPP services during the same period of time, or if you are one of a number of people who provide EPP services to a client on a rotating or shared basis, you may be an independent contractor. Another test is how you are paid. If your principal deducts tax and other amounts from your paycheck, you are likely an employee, but if you are paid a fixed amount and are expected to pay your own taxes as a private businessperson, you may be an independent contractor. A final test is how much control the principal has on how you do your job. This issue of being an agent or independent contractor matters in two major ways—liability and business. In regards to liability, you may be sued for causing damage or harm to someone or for payment of services or goods you ordered on behalf of your principal. If you are an agent, the principal will likely be liable for payment. If you are an independent contractor, you will be liable for payment of these lawsuits. If you are an independent contractor, you will need to make sure you have liability insurance to cover yourself for things that may occur in the performance of your job. In respect to business, if you are an independent contractor you must establish and operate your own business. This includes such details as licenses, registrations, taxes, and other business procedures.

LICENSE REQUIREMENTS

Whether you are an agent or an independent contractor, it is your responsibility to ensure that you obtain all the required licenses to perform your job and to keep them current and valid. The licenses you require and the procedures to obtain them will vary greatly from state to state, and we can only give you some guidelines on what to expect. Generally you will require three types of licenses: a professional license, a firearm or concealed-carry license or permit, and a driver license.

You will likely require a license to practice your profession. This license may be set out in your state law as a license for a private investigator or security guard since the profession of executive protection is fairly small, even though it is a growing one. The requirements to obtain a license may include completion of courses and a period of internship or working with a fully licensed person or agency. In Florida, for example, it can take two years or more to become fully licensed. You will possibly be required to take periodic upgrading courses and will be required to renew your license on a regular basis.

If you don't bother to get a license because you think, "I'm just going to protect this one person and don't need a license," you may get away with it, but you run the risk of being detained or having charges brought against you if the authorities determine that you are practicing without a license. This can be embarrassing for you to explain to your principal or, worse, can leave your principal unprotected while you sort out your personal legal problems. The time you will be caught for not having a license will be when you are involved in an accident, fight, dispute, or shooting because law enforcement will be involved. You will also be required to produce a valid license to practice your profession when you request a firearm license or permit, and possibly when you request a special classification of driver license.

If you are going to carry a firearm as part of your job, you will need the proper license or permit to carry a concealed firearm while performing this job of executive protection. A civilian concealed-carry license or permit is not sufficient. These civilian licenses are only for the self-defense of a person, and generally the law specifies that they are not for employment purposes, even though a person is generally allowed to carry his or her concealed firearm to work for his or her own personal protection. Don't rely on your civilian concealed-carry license or permit for your executive protection job duties. You could put that license in jeopardy if you misuse it. There will be a provision that allows you to obtain a firearms license specifically to perform your job duties. You will need to take the required courses and obtain this specific license or permit. This license, like the civilian one, will allow you to carry a firearm for the specific purposes of your job, but won't allow you to carry the firearm when you are off duty for your own protection, so it is best, where possible, to get both licenses.

Remember that firearms licenses are generally valid only within the state that issues them. Most states will not allow a person with a civilian concealed-carry license from another state to carry. For professional firearms licenses there are reciprocal provisions by which states will recognize the professional concealed-carry license from another state, but states may require that you get prior written authorization. You should check well in advance of travel to another state on what its requirements are and make sure you have all the proper documentation that will allow you to carry a firearm in that state. If you are going to another country, plan on taking six months or more to receive approval to take or carry a firearm. Some countries, like Canada, for instance, won't allow you to bring a handgun into the country no matter what type of license you may have. Be prepared. You don't want to get stopped at customs and arrested in a foreign country for a firearms violation and thus leave your principal completely unprotected.

Another important feature of professional firearms licenses and permits is that they may restrict you to certain types or calibers of handguns. In Florida, for example, certain classes of professional firearms licenses restrict the person to .38 caliber factory ammunition only. Rarely, if ever, will you get a license to carry a fully automatic firearm. Never carry anything more than your license or permit allows.

You should get the highest level of driver license that you may need. You never know when you might need to drive a bus or large vehicle in a special circumstance, so you should be prepared with the proper driver license. Keep your driver license clean and don't get demerits or restrictions on your driver license because of driving violations.

LIABILITY

You will be legally liable for your acts as an EPP. However, if you can show an agency relationship with your principal, your principal may be responsible to pay damages for civil suits brought against you for injury or damage caused in the course of doing your job. The best way to deal with legal liability is to avoid doing anything that will result in damage or a lawsuit.

If you commit a crime while acting as an EPP, you will be solely responsible. A criminal act, even by an agent, does not shift liability to the principal. Of course, if the principal was a party to the crime or a coconspirator, he or she will be criminally liable for his or her own participation in the crime. Crime involves every illegal act from murder to speeding. If you commit a crime, you will be liable and will have to be responsible for any penalty that is imposed by a court. It won't be a valid defense that you were protecting your principal.

In the area of civil liability there are three areas of law that may result in liability to you or your principal: contract, intentional torts, and negligence. Contract law involves such things as renting vehicles and equipment, making purchases, booking hotel and meeting rooms, and the like. If you make any such arrangements for your principal, generally the principal will be liable to pay for these. For the most part, there will not be a problem with this. If, however, you don't discuss some special equipment or some activity that you think that you should do, and you make arrangements for the equipment or activity, you may be liable for the payment. For example, you are going to a different city and you think that you should have extra people patrol outside the hotel and meeting rooms. You phone a friend of yours who is an EPP in that city and get him to arrange for people to patrol outside the hotel and meeting rooms on a 24-hour basis. You have never done this before, but you don't tell your principal about it. Later, when your EPP friend sends you a bill for the service of his agents, your principal could refuse to pay on the basis that he didn't authorize this unusual expenditure that was outside the normal scope of your employment. For anything unusual or extra, always get the prior approval of your principal. You should do this so he or she will authorize the expenditure, and so he or she will be aware of the type of protection you are providing and know what is going on in general.

Intentional torts (tort is a legal word that means civil wrong) include acts that a person does intentionally that cause hurt or damage to another. For example, things such as battery and trespass are intentional torts. If you commit an intentional tort (you trespass by going into someone's property without permission to look for potential hidden attackers, or you grab someone who is approaching your principal), you can be sued by the person for money damages. The lawsuit will name both you and your principal. If an agency relationship exists and if you were authorized by your principal to commit the act resulting in the lawsuit, your principal will possibly be liable to pay the damages. However, if your principal did not authorize you to commit the act, you may be personally liable to pay any damages awarded by the court. This is a very complex area of law, and the outcome will depend on many factors. Your best defense is to avoid behavior and actions that may result in the commission of intentional torts, which, of course, is a difficult thing for someone engaged in the protection of another.

Negligence is another complex area of law that may result in a lawsuit being brought against you and your principal. Negligence liability can result when three elements are present: (1) there must be a duty of care not to cause harm, (2) you must breach that duty of care, and (3) damage must result from the breach. An example is that we all have a general duty of care not to injure other people. If you drive recklessly in a motor vehicle in heavy traffic or where there are many pedestrians, this may be a breach of that duty of care. If you don't hit anyone and there is no damage, there is no problem, but if you do hit someone and cause some damage, you will be liable in negligence law to pay for that damage.

In an agency relationship, generally a principal will not authorize an employee to act negligently, and so such actions may be outside the scope of employment. However, in an executive protection situation you will generally be authorized to drive fast or do other acts that are necessary to get your principal out of danger. If you cause damage in doing this and are sued and found liable in negligence, your principal may be liable to pay the damages. If the action involves a motor vehicle, it is likely your principal who will have the insurance to cover payment of the damages.

It is important to remember that just because you are licensed to protect your principal, you are not immune from criminal or civil legal liability for your acts. Too often movies show chase scenes where cars smash through street vendor's carts, throwing fruit and vegetables high into the air, crash into other vehicles and push them out of the way, and knock down buildings and fences. What the movies don't show are the lawsuits against the drivers of the chasing cars from each of the people who have suffered loss or damage, the years of litigation, and the payment of damages to everyone who suffered a loss.

6

Keeping the Principal away from Danger

The best way to protect your principal is to keep him or her out of harm's way. This chapter covers some basic guidelines that you can utilize to aid you in accomplishing this task. The Appendix provides some sample checklists that you can use for organizing the protection of your principal. Always remember that meticulous planning and forethought will prevent problems and enhance your reputation as a professional. If your principal is exposed to danger because of your lack of intelligence gathering or due to poor planning, you will still end up looking like a dunce, even if you pull a rescue out of your hat. There are no excuses for poor performance in this business. You are either competent or you are not. The outcome of any work you do will hinge on the quality of your planning and preparation.

SECRECY

One of your best tools in protecting your principal is secrecy. The ability to keep your principal's "routine" as unroutine as possible is essential. The less others know about your principal's activities, the safer he or she will be. The less predictable his or her activities are, the smaller the opportunity will be for an intruder to plan a way to get to your principal.

It is critically important that only those with a need to know have information about your principal and his or her itinerary. As well, intelligence information that you gather should be released only on a need-to-know basis. Sometimes the most casual or innocent remarks, made in passing, can give an intruder that one bit of information necessary to create a window of opportunity. The old World War II saying "Loose lips sink ships" is certainly true in the executive protection field. All information regarding your principal should be considered valuable and confidential. If you avoid all unnecessary conversation with everyone (even other employees) about your principal and his or her family and associates, you reduce the chance that vital information will be inadvertently given out.

PROTECTIVE CORDONS

In order to keep your principal from encountering a confrontation, you may wish to establish cordons of protection. This is only possible when one is working as part of a detail. This will help to make protection and moving of your principal safer and more secure.

Cordons of protection can be broken down into the outer, middle, and inner cordons. Each provides a layer of protection and security that reinforces the others.

1. The outer cordon (or group of people formed around a person or place) is made up of control centers, response teams, snipers, observation posts, and the like. These are designated to provide a visible deterrent as well as having a response and tactical purpose.
2. The middle cordon includes search teams, intrusion detection teams, EPPs with metal detectors, bomb-sniffing dogs, and other technical people to enhance security.
3. The inner cordon is the team of immediate close-in detail members, including the personal security officer (PSO)/EPP and other close-formation members.

GROUND TRAVEL

Even the simplest activities, such as walking from one building to another, have inherent risk. If you have chosen to accept high-risk assignments (a principal who has many enemies or high risk and exposure), this is especially true. The EPP recognizes these risks and is ever vigilant in reducing or eliminating them. If you are a single agent, your task is often more difficult. Walking with your principal may appear to be a harmless activity. In fact, it is a high-risk activity. With no building, car, plane, or train around him or her, your principal is truly exposed.

Do not limit your perception of threat to an intruder. There are many other possible dangers as well. It is your function to be sure that your principal is not hit crossing an intersection, or that he or she does not slip on a patch of ice, snow, or wet grass. You must be careful in your planning when there is the possibility of falling objects (e.g., near a construction site) or a vicious stray dog in a residential neighborhood. You must be prepared with an umbrella in the event of rain. Your principal's protection from everyday accidents and his or her comfort are equally as important as the threat from intruders.

When you are walking down the street, be certain to shield your principal by placing yourself between your principal and his or her most exposed side. Be leery of corners or any opening or shadow that could hide potential danger. As well, you must routinely check behind you. Be sure to place equal value on keeping yourself out of harm's way. This is not a contradiction to your job description, but supports it. If you are injured or killed, guess who is next. If someone attacks you (the EPP), it is most likely that his or her motive is to get you out of the way in order to get to your principal. This is one good argument for maintaining a low profile. If you are obviously the bodyguard, you may be the first target of an attack in order to clear the way to your principal.

Walking safely with your principal is more easily accomplished with a security detail. There is strength in numbers. Not only do you have the ability to cover more windows of opportunity, you also have an evacuation advantage. Certain members on your detail should have the designated job of delaying the intruder while others on the detail attend to evacuating the principal. If you are working alone, evacuate the principal at the first reasonable opportunity. Remember that it is not your job to stay and fight. It is your job to get your principal to safety.

Avoid crowds whenever possible. If you must be in a crowd for some reason, scan the crowd visually at about elbow height. You will not see a weapon come out if you are looking at people's faces. You may have to be a bit pushy once in a while (in the politest manner possible, of course), but never let anyone from the crowd get between you and your principal. If necessary, take hold of your principal's arm or place your hand on his or her shoulder. This indicates to others that you are together. Generally, people will respect this and allow you to pass together if they are aware of this.

MOTORCADES

When you are organizing a motorcade, the following should be considered:

1. Driver selection
2. Vehicle selection
3. Vehicle preparation and search
4. Route planning
5. Attack and recognition drills and evade and escape drills

Driver Selection

It is a big advantage if the drivers you select are either members of your detail or have some type of security background. Especially with mid- or high-risk assignments, a detailed background check should be done on the drivers of each vehicle, especially the principal's driver. If time permits, go with the driver during a test run and observe how he drives as well as his powers of observation. It is a great advantage if each driver is familiar with the local area, language, and customs.

Vehicle Selection

In choosing the proper vehicle, consider your needs. The size, model, and look are important. If you are attempting to maintain a low profile, you certainly would not want to select a shocking pink stretch limousine. If your principal is expecting companion travelers, you would not want to show up driving a Corvette. In many cases this decision won't be yours to make. The vehicle you must use may belong to your principal or to his or her company. When the choice is given to you, examine your needs and purpose and then select the proper vehicle.

Vehicle Preparation and Search

Vehicle search does not refer only to looking for foreign objects. It also means checking to make sure that everything in the vehicle is in working order. It requires such tasks as checking the oil and other fluid levels and tire inflation. You would be embarrassed (not to mention unemployed) if your principal's car broke down because you neglected something as simple as checking the oil. You must be certain that the lug wrench is with the spare tire and that it is the one that really goes with the car. Check to see that the spare tire is properly inflated and that the jack is in the car in the event of a flat. Make sure that the windows, doors, and door locks are all in proper working order. Check to see when the vehicle was last serviced. If it is a long trip, remember to include food, water, or any other amenities that your principal might require. Remember the first-aid kit, and see that the communication equipment is working properly.

You will also need to know who has had access to the vehicle. You will want to know if anyone has had the opportunity to place anything in any vehicle without your knowledge. In mid- and high-risk assignments you will want to search for bugs and/or bombs. Look for signs of vehicle tampering that an amateur might leave like oily hand marks on the hood or trunk or pry or scratch marks near door, trunk, or hood locks. This will be covered in greater detail in the chapter on auto search.

Route Planning

It is important that you have a secure route planned. As well, you should have mapped out at least two alternate routes and a safe haven. In an emergency evacuation it is important to leave the area of danger, but you must also have somewhere to go when you leave. This place is called the safe haven. A safe haven is selected so that the PSO/EPP will know in advance where to evacuate the principal to. The reason for the alternate routes can be for anything from a fallen tree in the road, an accident that has blocked traffic, or encountering road construction or a parade to an attack or abduction attempt against your principal. Things like a parade should not interfere if you have done your advance homework.

Remember that the shortest route is not always the best route. As well, don't take the same route every time on routine trips such as going to the principal's office and home. Pick safe routes that leave you options in the case of an emergency. Both you and the driver should know the location of area hospitals and law-enforcement stations.

Attack and Recognition Drills and Evade and Escape Drills

Whenever time permits, and that won't always be the case, subject your detail to mock accident and intruder scenarios. If each detail member knows exactly what he or she should do in an emergency, the process will go much more smoothly. It is said that practice makes perfect. That is only partially true. Only perfect practice makes perfect. That is certainly true in the executive protection field.

Motorcade Structure

A motorcade will normally consist of two or more vehicles. Ideally, it will have three or more vehicles. These vehicles will include the lead vehicle containing other detail members, the principal's vehicle, and the follow vehicle. If there are only two cars available, the lead vehicle is usually the one to be eliminated unless there are extenuating circumstances that dictate otherwise. If there are additional vehicles in the motorcade, the follow car may in turn be followed by one or more staff cars and a tail car (see figure 6.1). If the motorcade is being led by police escort or another security escort, the police car in front of the lead car of your group of vehicles is called the pilot car (see figure 6.2). If the press is involved or if there are guests in the motorcade, these cars are placed behind the staff cars and in front of the tail car.

The lead car should carry a driver and other detail members such as the advance man and, if needed, a specially trained and armed escort. This powerfully armed individual is sometimes called the bagman. The bagman generally carries an attaché case containing a semiautomatic weapon or, in some situations involving dignitary protection, a fully automatic firearm that has greater firepower than the handguns other agents might carry.

The principal's car should carry the driver and the EPP assigned as the personal security officer or agent to accompany the principal in the front seat. The principal should travel in the back seat. In high-risk situations another detail member may also be assigned to ride in the back seat with the principal.

The follow car's purpose is to be a blocking agent. It should carry the driver, the shift leader, and other detail members. The staff in the lead car should always be on the lookout for any out-of-the-ordinary activity near the motorcade. The driver of the principal's vehicle should follow closely enough to the lead car so as not to allow another vehicle to come between that vehicle and the lead car, yet far enough to allow maneuvering space. The follow car should follow closely enough not to allow any other vehicle to get between that vehicle and the principal's car (see figure 6.3).

In some cases you may also choose to include decoy vehicles as part of the motorcade. This refers to a decoy car that others might suspect carries your principal that is dispatched, possibly with its own motorcade, to draw attention away from the actual principal car and/or motorcade.

Figure 6.4 shows an example of common motorcade activity. Upon reaching any destination, the lead car and follow car deploy their detail members first. The advance man (from the lead car) moves back toward the principal's car and prepares to take "the point." This assumes that an advance man was not sent ahead to receive the entourage. If an advance man has been dispatched ahead, he or she should be visible to the motorcade as it approaches. Unless he or she gives a prearranged signal that it is okay for the motorcade to stop, it will continue on without stopping until it is cleared for arrival by the advance man.

The armed escort, or another detail member if there is no armed escort, will exit his vehicle on the open-road side of the car. As well, a detail member in the follow car will exit on the open-road side. They will both move toward the principal's car and take positions near the front and rear fenders (road side of vehicle). The shift leader

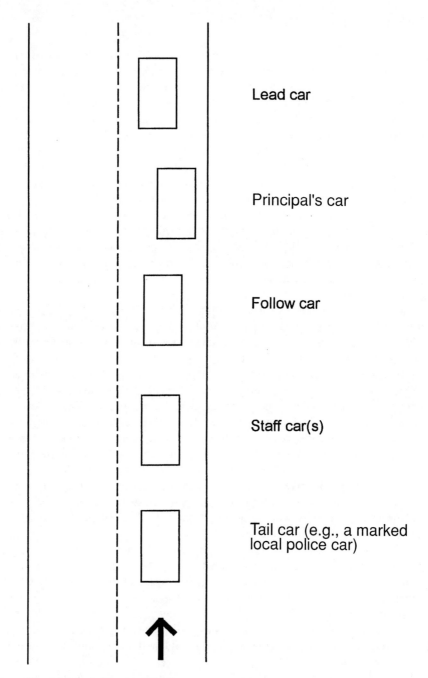

Figure 6.1   Motorcade Routine Travel

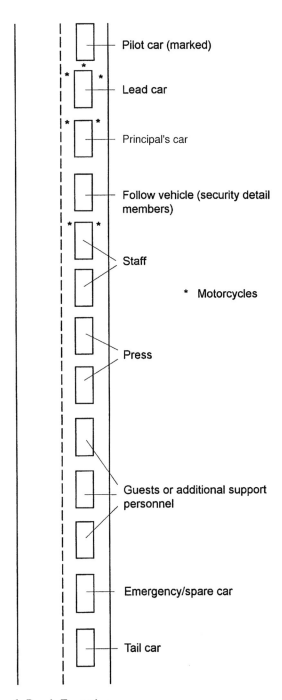

Figure 6.2   Motorcade Parade Formation

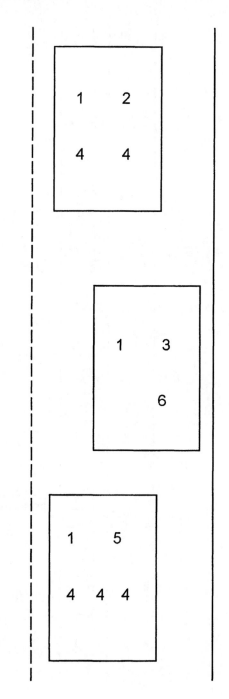

Figure 6.3   Deployment Positions

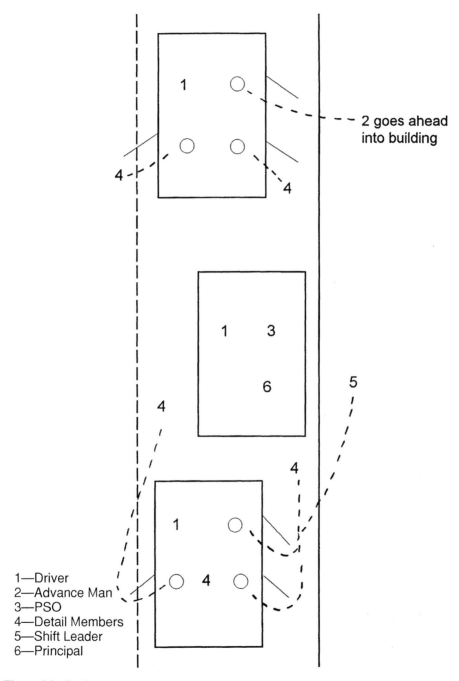

2 goes ahead
into building

1—Driver
2—Advance Man
3—PSO
4—Detail Members
5—Shift Leader
6—Principal

Figure 6.4   Deployment

(follow car) and other detail members from both the lead and follow cars will exit their vehicles and take similar positions curbside. When all agents are in position, and the area has been secured, the advance man will signal the PSO/EPP, and the PSO/EPP will signal the principal that it is safe to exit the vehicle. The detail will then take positions in a formation around the principal and escort him or her into the building or other destination.

Generally speaking, the most dangerous part of auto travel is when your principal is entering or exiting a vehicle. When exiting a building to board a vehicle, your principal should be kept in safety, perhaps in a secured room, until his or her vehicle and the follow car are in position. Your principal's vehicle should be brought as close to the point of departure as possible. Then and only then should you escort your principal to the vehicle. The pickup should always be done in such a way that your principal does not have to enter a roadway to get into his or her vehicle. In other words, don't park across the street. If the street is busy and parking is a problem, your advance man can sometimes place cones in front of the building when the first available parking slots become available. If not, you may be forced to form a second row of cars (double-park) for the very few seconds that it should take to move your principal from the building to the vehicle. In any event, don't make your principal cross the street.

A great deal of your preparation and planning must revolve around the event of moving from location to location. This is the time during travel that your principal is most exposed. The exact time and place of arrival should be known only to those with a need to know.

AIR TRAVEL

Again, planning is the key for both the safety and comfort of your principal. It is important that you be familiar with the type of aircraft that you and your party will fly on. Make airline reservations well in advance. Plan security both en route and at the airport. Ground transportation must be attended to in advance for both ends of the trip. Carefully plan how you will handle luggage. It is your job as an EPP to be certain that all of this comes together without a hitch.

When you are making reservations for your principal, his or her family, and friends and associates, reserve the flights as far in advance as possible so that you can get the seats that you want. This will allow you not only to secure better seats but better prices too. Price may or may not be a consideration to your principal, but seating is always important to you both.

Use your name or the name of the company as the customer or contact person with any travel agent. Do not use your principal's name on anything except his or her ticket. In the past, it was common practice not to use the principal's name on the ticket either. Due to increased security over the past few years, and the need to present individual identification at the airport, this is not usually an option anymore. Following these steps, however, will help your principal maintain a lower profile.

Find out what seats the people traveling in your principal's party prefer. Some may like a window, some an aisle, and so forth. Obtain a seating chart of the aircraft, or if that is not possible, review the seating chart with the travel agent. Make sure that you and any detail members traveling with you are strategically seated around your principal in order to provide the maximum coverage for your principal. Consider, as well, access to emergency exits. This will make your job easier in the event of an attack or a natural or mechanical emergency.

Basic motorcade protocol will apply when going to or from an airport. If possible, after arrival at the airport, and if your principal has the clout, arrange to hold your principal in a security room prior to the flight. Do everything that you can to arrange for your principal to board early, even before the rest of the first-class passengers and preferably through a secured entrance. If the entrance gate is exposed, arrange to drive the principal onto the tarmac for preboarding. In this way he or she can enter the aircraft with the smallest amount of contact with others in the airport. This has become more difficult in the United States with today's increasingly stringent Federal Aviation Administration (FAA) rules, but it is still worth the effort if you can arrange it.

It is the "kiss of death" (unemployment) to lose your principal's or his or her spouse's luggage. Be sure to make luggage routing as idiot-proof as possible. Also, you or other security detail members should carry on some important articles, such as toiletries and a change of clothes, for your principal and companions whenever possible. Whether loss of luggage is your fault or that of a careless bellhop, you will probably get the heat for the loss.

Make certain that all luggage is clearly marked at the airport to meet U.S. or foreign requirements. When possible, use your name, a code name, or a company name on all bags. Do not use your principal's name on baggage if you can get around it. You may be able to tag luggage in your or other detail members' names while in the airport instead of your principal's. Remove all tags showing individual names as soon as you leave the airport. Bags should show the least possible information while in transit. As long as a contact number and hotel address are visible in the event that a bag is lost, any other information should be omitted. Depend on color coding or some other method for identification of the luggage of individuals. Don't make it easy for someone to find a particular person's bag and slip something into it. A good method to use is simply to color-code each bag with a colored sticker or ribbon. Bellhops can simply be told, "Take the red tags to room 123 and the blue tags to room 124." On the luggage have a tag that gives a local or your cell phone number. For example, "If this bag is lost in [name of the city you will be traveling in], please call [phone number] as soon as possible." These tips will help to idiot-proof your luggage handling.

The resources available to your principal and the power he or she wields will have a direct impact on your security plans at an airport. The size of the airport also will make a difference. Smaller or private airports are easier to get concessions from. Larger or international airports are usually less flexible. Especially in larger airports, solicit as much help as possible from the airport security. Don't be competitive with those who can assist you. Learn to work with other security units, and all will benefit.

RAIL TRAVEL

Rail is not one of the preferred means of travel, especially for short distances where it is unlikely that one will be able to get a private berth. Although some countries have rail systems that provide greater privacy and flexibility, it is still much harder to provide security in most situations when traveling by rail. If you must travel by rail, attempt to do the following:

1. Whenever possible, obtain a private berth.
2. If a berth is not available, choose seating where the seats or benches face each other. It is preferable if one of these seats is against the wall at the end of the car.
3. Draw the window shade when the train is stopped.
4. Sit near an exit.
5. Don't mingle your or your principal's luggage with that of other passengers.
6. Know where all of the regular exits and emergency exits are.
7. Know where the emergency-brake cable or alarm is located.
8. Arrange seating so that your principal has the least exposure to others and to unsecured areas.
9. If your detail is large enough, place an EPP at both ends of the car to observe those entering and exiting.
10. Choose a car that is close to the dining/club car (if you will need to use it) so that it is not necessary for you to pass through unsecured cars to get to that car.
11. As with the airport, try to have access to a secured room for your principal after he or she arrives at the train station and before departure. If this is not possible, it is best to have him or her remain in the car (preferably in motion) until the last possible moment.
12. Reserve seats in advance when possible. If that particular train does not have reserved seating, have an EPP or small detail get to the station before your principal and secure the most appropriate seats.
13. Have an advance man (or advance detail) waiting at your point of arrival.
14. Be on alert any time that the train stops to take on or discharge passengers.

These steps will help to minimize your principal's exposure. Generally less preferred than train travel (from a security standpoint) is a public bus or a bicycle. In some instances chartering a private bus might be a better alternative than rail travel.

BUILDING ENTRANCE AND EXIT

For maximum protection and efficiency, it is important to know the layout of any buildings and grounds that you will be visiting. There are two primary ways of accomplishing this. One is to obtain blueprints of each building and its immediate surroundings. The other is to send an advance person or team to physically explore the destination location. Whenever possible, both should be done. This holds especially true in high-risk or security-sensitive assignments.

Advancing a building location may be difficult or impossible if you are a single agent. This leaves you with the option of reviewing the original (and any additional or newer) building plans. It is always good to review the original plans of a building first. You should then compare these drawings with any new blueprints of additions or new mechanical installations such as air conditioners and duct work, plumbing, and the like to locate anything that may have become obscured in the subsequent drawings. If landscaping plans are available, you will need to review them as well.

If you are able to advance a building, it will give you an entirely different perspective of the surroundings. The difference between looking at the blueprints of a building and physically being in the building is analogous to that between seeing a person's X rays and visiting with that person. If you want to get the complete picture, it is best to do both. By advancing the building, you will gather additional information not seen on building plans. You will know the placement of movable fixtures, pay phones, furniture, and so forth. You can see the exits and entrances firsthand and note the location of fire extinguishers and other equipment. You can also speak personally with staff or building security. Be sure to include parking lots and garages as part of your intelligence gathering and advance work. This information is critical to planning safe corridors of entry and exit.

Let us assume that you are en route to a building that you have advanced. Let us further assume that you have an advance agent on the premises. What procedure would you use to safely move your principal from the motorcade to the building?

A member of the advance team should be at the entrance where your principal will disembark, and be in view of the motorcade. Subtle, prearranged signals between drivers and the advance team should have already been agreed on. These should include one signal that it is okay to stop, one to make another pass, and one to abort the drop and continue on without stopping. If the building and grounds are not secured, the motorcade should not stop.

When approaching the destination building, the principal's vehicle should always pull curbside on the side of the street where the building is located. This is so your principal never has the need to enter the roadway. If there is a follow car, it should stagger its position so that it is jutting out slightly into the road more than the principal's vehicle, thereby filling its job as a blocking agent. At this time the security detail should exit the vehicle(s) and take positions as outlined in the motorcade section of this chapter.

The principal should be moved without hesitation and as quickly as is safely possible into the building. Keep weather conditions and the terrain in mind. If you have done your intelligence gathering properly, you will know the location of the room that you are going to occupy and the most secure route within the building to get there. You will have established alternate routes and escape routes just as you would with a motorcade in the event of a problem.

If hotel registration or other paperwork needs to be done it should be completed in one of the following ways: (1) Have the room(s) reserved in advance in a name other than the principal's. Leave a member of the detail who has been designated for this duty to complete any paperwork. (2) If you are a single EPP, make reservations, in advance, in your name. When you arrive, advise the host that you would like to see the principal safely to his room and that you will then return to the desk to sign the necessary papers. You may also arrange to have the papers brought to you at your room(s) in order that you do not need to leave your principal. This is the best option if your host will cooperate. They normally will have no problem in accommodating you, especially if arrangements have been made in advance. If you cannot arrange to go to your room before registering, have your principal fill out the register while you keep watch. As soon as you are registered, get the key and go directly to your principal's room. Your principal's and your luggage should never leave your sight. Never let the bellperson go ahead with the luggage or bring it later.

Suppose that you are en route with your principal as a single agent. You have done your intelligence gathering, have reviewed the blueprints of buildings and grounds, and have possibly even visited the building. The only difference is that you have no detail members to share the workload with. How do you get your principal safely into the building? Consider the following suggestions:

1. If you are driving a car, try to utilize facilities that have valet parking.
2. If there is no valet parking, an enclosed garage (preferably with security) is next best.
3. If you have been successful at creating a positive relationship with building security, you should attempt to solicit their assistance. You may be able (by way of cellular phone or radio) to have them act in the capacity of an advance person.
4. As long as you are confident in the company, you may want to book a limousine to go to any meetings. I (Philip Holder) personally am a little leery about doing this because I have no way of knowing how stringent their security is in preventing access to the vehicle in my absence or how well the driver has been screened. It is, however, an option that you may want to consider.

If you must enter an unsecured area (parking lot, unsupervised garage, or the like) with little or no assistance, your best weapon is secrecy. Your route and exact time of arrival should only be known to those with an urgent need to know. These privileged people should be politely directed to keep that information confidential as well.

Exiting a building is for the most part a reversal of entering. When you are working with a detail, the principal should be kept in safety until the motorcade arrives. Seconds prior to the motorcade arriving curbside, the PSO should be notified by radio or cellular phone. When the motorcade is ready to accept the principal, he or she should be quickly escorted, without hesitation, to the principal's vehicle. The motorcade should depart without hesitation.

If you are a single operative, you have the same problems at exit as with entry. Whenever possible, enlist the help of building security people whom you know and trust. You can't be all places at once, so get help where you can. Remember at the same time that unreliable or untrustworthy help can be more of a threat than no help at all. You must weigh the pros and cons on an individual case-by-case basis.

7

Packages and Luggage

There are many times each day that you and your principal may have the need to access luggage and packages. Each time you do so presents an inherent danger.

RECEIVING AND/OR FINDING PACKAGES

Good things come in small packages. So do loud explosions. This is why inspection of packages is important, especially in high-risk assignments and/or when your principal is involved in emotionally charged issues such as abortion, the environment, or religion. Today, almost anyone can be the target of random violence. Always be on guard.

Since we will describe search procedures in chapters 11 and 12, "Auto Search" and "Building Search," we will not duplicate that information by discussing how to find bombs or devices in a building. We will focus on specific procedures and what to look for when a package is found or received.

MAIL

When mail is received, it should always be inspected prior to its being given to your principal. The following are some mail and package procedures that will help to provide for the safety of your principal:

1. See if your principal will agree to allow you to open and inspect all mail and packages. If you have built the necessary trust with your principal, he or she often will agree. Assure your principal that you will not violate his or her privacy by reading or going through this mail. You will only go as far as to look for signs of something that could be suspect. Tell your principal that you would prefer, as part of your job, to take such risk on the principal's behalf. If the principal will not agree to this, then you must screen the mail and packages to the best of your ability while they are still unopened.
2. Look for the absence of a return address or for a suspicious return address.
3. Listen for sounds emanating from packages.
4. Look for signs of oily residue often associated with certain types of explosives that may be left on envelopes or the wrapping of a package.

5. Look for restrictive markings such as "personal," "confidential," or "only for." Attempts to avoid security checks and to get a package directly to your principal should be viewed as suspicious.

6. Excessive postage is often used on such packages to be sure that they reach their destination. It is also to assure that they are not held at the post office or that the post office does not attempt to return them to a fictitious return address. Also, postage may be in the form of many postage stamps instead of one metered stamp. This might be so that the sender does not have to go to the postal counter, where he or she might later be identified by a counter person.

7. Give extra caution to foreign, air, or special-delivery packages.

8. Handwritten addresses in block or childlike writing or poorly typed or written addresses should be suspect.

9. Look for misspelling of common words.

10. A letter addressed to a person's title, without a name, should be scrutinized.

11. Be suspicious if the package seems unusually heavy for its size.

12. Be suspicious of an uneven or lopsided package.

13. If you feel any wires or suspicious lumps through an envelope or package, approach with caution.

14. An excessively rigid envelope is cause for concern.

15. Be suspicious of packages with excessive amounts of tape, string, or other packaging material that may conceal a trip wire or other detonating device. Such material may also conceal packing used to increase the intensity of an explosion.

If you discover a package on the premises that has any of these characteristics or if you receive such a package in the mail, you have two options, depending on the degree of your concern. One is to open the package; the other is to call in law enforcement trained in bomb recognition and disarming. We recommend that you contact law enforcement if you feel that there is cause for concern. It is better to be embarrassed by a false alarm than to be blown to bits. If you elect to open a suspicious package, get some hands-on training from a bomb expert first. The following are some basic procedures for opening such packages that are normally discussed in such courses:

1. Open windows and doors; clear area back 300 feet.

2. Lay the package on a flat table or counter.

3. Open the package slowly and carefully, looking for trip wires, tin foil, or other suspicious items. If another detail member is present, have that member (or members) observe from various angles, just as with auto search.

4. Have something of sufficient weight ready to place on partially opened package flaps to prevent them from opening further should you detect some type of device meant to detonate an explosive when the package is opened.

5. If such a device is found, weight the open flap, place a mattress or some explosion-absorbing item in front of the package, and evacuate the area. Do not attempt to defuse a device yourself. That is not your job. Call in the proper authorities who have the proper training and equipment for the job.

GIFTS

There are times when someone may attempt to approach your principal with a "gift." It is important that no one be able to get near to your principal with unexamined packages. Keep in mind that the package may truly be a gift. For this reason, diplomacy must be used in redirecting the gift giver. You may need to direct him or her away, saying that now is just not a good time for the exchange. Offer to see to it that your principal will receive the gift. Get the person's name and any other pertinent information. Give the package to a detail member who is free to examine the package if you are not. If you are working alone, have the package put in a secure area until such time as you are able to examine it.

If the gift giver refuses to leave the package or give his or her name, report this suspicious activity to law-enforcement authorities. If you or another detail member can do so without putting your principal at risk, follow the person and get a tag number, auto description, and any other information that may make it easier to identify and locate the individual later.

LUGGAGE

It is important that luggage always be kept secured. This includes your principal's briefcase, purse, laptop computer, and so forth. If it is impossible to have the luggage secured at all times, consider the following tips. One way to detect signs of tampering is by placing a tape or wax seal in some inconspicuous place on the luggage. You can also set luggage combination locks to specific numbers that you record. If the numbers have changed or the seal has been broken, you have reason to suspect tampering. If the luggage has a key lock, rub soap or wax into the keyhole to make a seal. If the lock seal is broken, be suspicious. If tampering occurs, use the same principles described in auto and package search to determine the course of action to be taken with the luggage. If a person gains access to your principal's luggage, it can result in physical, emotional, and/or economic damage. Luggage is a location in which both eavesdropping and explosive devices may be concealed.

You may need to check luggage at airports. From this point on, the luggage is, for your intent and purpose, unsecured. A couple suggestions are to put wax or soap in the keyhole of the luggage locks or insert a slip of cloth or paper in the edge of the suitcases. Upon receiving the luggage, I check to see if this has been disturbed. If you have any suspicions about luggage tampering, search the luggage. You may want to have all luggage transported in one of the other cars in your motorcade instead of in your principal's vehicle if possible.

8

Defensive Driving

To the EPP, "defensive driving" takes on an entirely different meaning than it has for the average driver. When you are a driver working as an EPP, there is far more to defensive driving than watching that the other driver doesn't run a red light. Although you must be aware of the everyday dangers present in driving, you must also be knowledgeable in many other areas. The following are some of the skills you will need:

1. Formation driving
2. Evasive driving (J-turns, bootlegs, Y-turns, threshold braking)
3. Running interference (primarily the follow car)
4. Vehicle emergency transfer (box formation)
5. Vehicle driving characteristics
6. Line of vision
7. Mechanical failure
8. Ramming

In this chapter we will cover the main academics of driving. Although you may be able to learn formations and some basics from other EPPs, the high-stress driving skills require much more training. To become a truly competent driver, we recommend that you enroll in a driving course under the supervision of a professional driver. I have taken this training, but we do not profess to be driving instructors. The instructor you choose for this very specialized training should first and foremost have a background in racecar driving and evasive driving. Preferably he or she should be someone who has some knowledge of the executive protection field and its specific driving needs. It is also important that he or she have access to a skid pad and a racetrack. There is no substitute for hands-on experience in learning these skills. You will need to actually get behind the wheel with an instructor. Never attempt to learn these techniques without a qualified instructor, and never practice these techniques in traffic or on public streets. This chapter will help you to prepare for that hands-on training experience with the instructor of your choice.

FORMATION DRIVING

If you have read the section on motorcades, you should already have a basic concept of vehicle formations. Now it is important to get some practical experience in these areas.

43

One thing that should be included in your training is practical drills. When you are enrolling in a driving course, ask your prospective instructor if these or similar drills are included in the program that you will be given.

Sample Drill 1

One vehicle will be designated as the attack vehicle. Two or more vehicles can be designated as the principal's vehicle, the follow vehicle, and, if available, other motorcade vehicles. As the motorcade moves along the course, the attack vehicle will approach on a course perpendicular to that of the principal's vehicle (simulating an intersection), attempting to intercept the principal's vehicle. What do you do?

Upon detecting the attack vehicle, the principal's vehicle should brake. The follow vehicle should accelerate and pass the principal's vehicle, thereby placing the follow vehicle between the attack car and the principal's vehicle. (All vehicles should be in radio contact at all times during the motorcade.) While this is going on, the PSO/EPP should go over the front seat into the rear seat of the principal's vehicle and push the principal down, shielding the principal with his or her own body. At this point the driver of the principal's vehicle should evacuate the area. He may use a J-turn (to be described later in this chapter) or similar maneuver in order to reverse direction. The follow vehicle (and other vehicles from the detail, if available) should run interference with the attack vehicle before following and rejoining the principal's vehicle.

Sample Drill 2

This drill focuses on entry and departure for the picking up and letting off of your principal. If your timing is right, the window of opportunity through which an attack could occur will be minimal. You will again need to designate an attack car and possibly a ground unit and/or a sniper as well. The attack team will attempt to penetrate defenses and gain access to the principal during the principal's move from the vehicle to a building. Your goal is to coordinate your resources in such a way that your principal is moved safely from the vehicle to a building without exposure or incident. This drill will help you to perfect your planning and timing in moving a principal from one location to another. It will also give you practice at organizing your detail so that everyone knows where he or she should be and what he or she should be doing during every second of the operation. If the attack team is successful, then you must reassess your planning and tactics.

Sample Drill 3

It may be necessary to avoid a roadblock set up to box in your principal. This drill will help you practice threshold braking and J-turns (discussed later in this chapter). The principal's car and follow car proceed in a straight line across the skid pad at 40 to 50 miles per hour. A roadblock should now be simulated by use of a predetermined point or upon a surprise cue. When this occurs, both vehicles must brake (threshold braking unless the cars are equipped with automatic braking system [ABS]). As soon as both vehicles are fully stopped, the drivers must put the vehicles in reverse, accelerate, and in synchronization perform simultaneous J-turns. As soon as both vehicles have made 180-degree turns, the principal's vehicle must accelerate, passing the follow car. With the follow car now behind the principal car (and between the principal and the supposed ambush), they can evacuate the area.

EVASIVE DRIVING

As stated earlier, practical driving skills must be taught hands-on by a qualified driving instructor. This section describes some of the evasive driving techniques you should expect to be instructed in at such a course.

J-Turn

You have probably seen J-turns in action films many times. As a car is speeding in reverse, the driver hits the brakes and cuts the wheel. Suddenly the vehicle spins around and takes off in the opposite direction. This is accomplished by accelerating in reverse to approximately 30 to 45 miles per hour. The driver then hits the brakes as he or she shifts quickly into drive. At the same time the driver turns the wheel sharply. As the car spins around and is facing forward in the opposite direction, the driver straightens out the wheel, lets up on the brake, and punches the accelerator to the floor. The car is now under full acceleration in the opposite direction.

Bootleg

A bootleg is accomplished when the driver hits the emergency brake (to lock up only the rear wheels) and cuts the steering wheel to one side. The rear of the vehicle will then slide around, and the vehicle will be facing the opposite direction. The emergency brake is used so that the front wheels can continue to rotate. If all four wheels were to lock, the vehicle would simply slide in the direction that it was originally headed.

Y-Turn

If the principal's vehicle should stop and reverse direction, possibly by use of a J-turn or bootleg, the follow car will come around and pass the principal's car (to place the follow car between an oncoming threat and the principal's vehicle) so that it is facing across the roadway. The follow car can then back up in order to face in the same direction as the principal's vehicle and then move forward behind the principal's vehicle, again resuming its position as a follow car.

Threshold Braking

Braking is most efficient when the wheels do not lock. This is the reason automatic braking system (ABS) braking was invented. Although many newer vehicles have ABS, you will need to know how to brake in the most effective way should you be in a vehicle not equipped with ABS. Locking up the wheels and sliding is 35 percent less effective for stopping and may put flat spots and unnecessary wear on tires. The result will be less control and loss of braking. The key to effective braking is to keep the tires rolling at all times until you can effectively stop without skidding. You will increase control of the vehicle and reduce braking distance once you master this skill.

These are some key points of threshold braking. Assume that your vehicle is traveling at 60 miles per hour and you need to make an emergency stop. With threshold braking you would do the following:

1. Hit the brakes hard and then immediately reduce the pressure on the brake pedal.
2. Adjust the pressure as the vehicle slows down.
3. Do not pump the brakes. Once the front end of the vehicle goes down (from the braking), you want to keep it down. If you pump the brakes, your vehicle will rock like a hobbyhorse and you will lose both control and braking efficiency.
4. When you hit the brakes, it is a good indicator if you hear a little "chirping" from the tires. If you hear a lot of squealing, you are applying the brakes too hard. Let up slightly on the brake pressure.
5. Your goal is to get the maximum degree of braking without locking the wheels.

RUNNING INTERFERENCE

It is primarily the follow car's job to act as a blocking agent and to run interference for the principal's vehicle. This is only used in a life-and-death situation where you have concluded that your principal is the target of violence and is in imminent danger. These tactics are not without serious risk to others, including your principal, yourself, pedestrians, and other vehicles.

If any vehicle outside of the detail attempts to forcibly interrupt the path of the principal's vehicle, pull up alongside the principal's vehicle, or get behind or in front of the principal's vehicle, this intruder vehicle must be blocked. In the event that an attack vehicle is in pursuit of the principal's vehicle, that vehicle must be detained in order to give the principal's vehicle time to evacuate the area. The responsibility for blocking is usually assigned to the follow vehicle.

VEHICLE EMERGENCY TRANSFER

In the event that the principal's vehicle is disabled or breaks down, you will need to transfer your principal to another vehicle in the motorcade. It will most likely be the lead vehicle, but of course that depends on the number of vehicles in the motorcade. The transfer must be secure for a number of reasons that include, but are not limited to, attack. You must also consider bad weather, accidental injury, and privacy (if your principal has celebrity status). One of the most common ways of accomplishing this is the box formation.

The box formation is quite simple. The car into which your principal will be moved will pull directly alongside of the principal's vehicle. The two vehicles should be close enough so that when the front and rear doors on both of the vehicles are open (we will assume that four-door vehicles are being used, as this is the standard), they will be close enough to each other to form a box between the two vehicles. In this way your principal can move from one vehicle to the other with the least amount of exposure. The doors of the vehicles in effect form walls or a box to protect the principal.

VEHICLE DRIVING CHARACTERISTICS

You will need to understand factors that affect vehicle dynamics. Weight distribution has a significant effect on vehicle handling. When a vehicle is in motion and going straight, an even amount of weight is present at all wheels. During braking, weight will transfer forward as the nose of the vehicle dips. During acceleration, weight will shift to the rear tires as the rear of the car lowers or the front rises. Weight management of the vehicle will determine how much the vehicle's vertical load will affect the contact patch of the tires. The contact patch is the area of the tire that actually is on the road at any particular time. Weight management and the contact patch of each tire will have a direct bearing on the stability of the vehicle.

You will also find that front-wheel-drive and rear-wheel-drive vehicles have slightly different driving characteristics. Many professional drivers differ in opinion as to which, if any, is preferred, but they are different. With rear-wheel drive, downshifting will slow down the rear wheels without loss of control by the front wheels. This is not true of front-wheel-drive vehicles. This is important because in order to maintain steering control, the front wheels of the vehicle must keep turning. If they stop turning and begin to slide, steering control is lost.

Front-wheel drive is often better in soft snow because the weight of the engine is over the drive wheels. This may be a benefit if you are in an area where snow is expected. Also, vehicles with front-wheel drive do not have the large hump in the floor that houses the drive shaft needed in rear-wheel-drive vehicles. These may all be considerations when selecting a vehicle. You should practice driving in both types of vehicles in order to feel comfortable driving either.

Understeer occurs when you turn the wheel of the vehicle, and instead of turning with good traction to the front wheels, the vehicle "plows" with the front wheels sliding. To correct this, decelerate, but do so slowly to avoid what is known as "trailing throttle oversteer." Oversteer occurs when the back end of the vehicle breaks free and swings around. This can happen when you accelerate or let up on the gas too quickly.

To remedy this, turn into the skid and take your foot off the accelerator, pause briefly, and then recover by straightening out the steering. Remember, when recovering from understeer or oversteer, your movements should be firm and quick but not abrupt and jerky. An overreaction may leave you in an even worse predicament than you originally encountered.

Tires play a big role in vehicle performance as well. A tire with a high temperature rating will probably hold up better during a high-speed evacuation. The lower the side wall of a tire, the more responsive it will be. The higher the side wall, the softer the ride will be. You may wish to factor in your principal's level of threat when purchasing tires for his or her vehicle(s). Often, drivers will increase the tire manufacturer's recommended inflation by five pounds in order to gain some extra stability from the tires. Consider the climate (hot, rainy, or whatever) when you select tires. Tread ratings, traction ratings, and temperature ratings should all be considered.

LINE OF VISION

Line of vision simply means that when you are driving, always look in the direction that you want to go. People tend to unwittingly steer in the direction that they are looking. Look through the window or path that you want to take, and you will be less likely to steer inappropriately.

MECHANICAL FAILURE

Another reason it is important to learn to do all driving maneuvers properly is to save wear and tear on your principal's vehicle. If you were to attempt a J-turn and in the process blow the vehicle's transmission, you would place your principal's life in jeopardy. Performing these maneuvers correctly will reduce the chance of vehicle and tire damage.

Should the principal's vehicle be damaged, remember that your principal's safety is the first concern. You can drive for quite a while (depending on the road surface) with a flat tire. A broken shock absorber will affect handling but will not incapacitate the vehicle totally. Your job is to evacuate your principal. Ruining a tire rim or damaging other parts of the vehicle is not important when compared to the safety of your principal. Let the follow car worry about the intruder. Get your principal out of harm's way.

RAMMING

As a last resort, ramming can be used to stop an intruder's vehicle. Of course, you won't want to practice this in the family car (for which your auto insurance agent will be grateful). Again, this would be the job of the follow car (or another motorcade vehicle). You do not want to chance disabling the principal's vehicle. If the need to ram occurs, attempt to use your front or rear bumper area against the front wheel well of the intruder's car. If the front wheel well is not accessible, aim at the rear wheel well. If you can take away the intruder's ability to steer, he will not be able to give chase. After disabling the intruder's vehicle, drive off. Remember, your job is to protect the principal. It is not to fight the bad guys.

9

Negotiation and Intelligence Gathering

Many potential problems and embarrassing situations can be avoided by negotiation. A fan insists that he needs an autograph right now. A person yells an insult or a veiled threat. An angry motorist complains because you stop your car in a no-parking zone. A tired traveler thinks that you are blocking his access to the exit or baggage claim. There are many situations where your interpersonal and negotiation skills can easily and quietly resolve a potential problem.

INTELLIGENCE GATHERING

Information is power. The more information you have, the better you will be able to look after your principal and do your job. You will need information for everything you do as an EPP, and you will constantly need to update this information.

Use every possible source of information. For example, if you are going to book rooms at a hotel you have never visited before, you can start by phoning the reservation desk. That will get you rooms, the hotel's location, phone numbers, and other facilities available, but you need much more than that. You need to know how many streets lead to the hotel, what the traffic pattern is like, how busy the hotel is, what types of people generally stay there, if there has been a crime problem at the hotel, if you can bring in your own catered food if needed, where the closest medical facilities are, how many entrances there are and if you can block one for your motorcade, where the stairs are in relation to the rooms you have, if there are "hiding places" or other potentially dangerous areas between the main doors and your rooms, how often the staff changes, if the hotel staff members have identification cards so you can recognize an impostor, what in-house security is available, and so on. You will need a similar amount of information about every aspect of each trip, activity, or day. You need information on airports, planes, vehicles, people, office buildings, roads, and other things. How will you get all this information?

Break down intelligence gathering into topics and resources. For example, to gather information about the hotel, your resources will include the hotel management, the doorman, maids, room-service personnel, local law enforcement, the city traffic office, the chamber of commerce, other EPPs who have used the hotel, your principal's other staff members, taxi drivers, and others. You can contact people by telephone, fax, mail, or e-mail. The best way to get information from "unofficial" people like maids, baggage handlers, or room-service delivery people is to talk to them one-on-one. Explain that you need their help, treat them like an equal, include them in your confidence, and tip them. You can often get more useful information from people on the front lines than from those in the head office.

Keep notes about what you learn. Don't overwhelm yourself with notes, but keep important things like people's names, phone numbers, and information that triggers something in your mind. You may not want to make notes in front of your informant. Many people don't like this, especially if they aren't in a job whose function is to give information. Make your notes as soon as possible, however, before you forget the details. If you have a team researching a building or trip, have a meeting after the intelligence gathering is completed to share information, determine what you are still missing, and make your plan. If you find that you get inconsistent information, recheck it with the original sources and try to get a new source to resolve the inconsistency and get the best information.

Intelligence gathering never ends. Always watch and listen for new information. Incorporate new information and revise your plan if needed.

NEGOTIATION AND INTELLIGENCE-GATHERING SKILLS

You also need good interpersonal and negotiation skills to be able to do your job as an EPP. You will need the cooperation and permission of hotel management, airport security, car rental agencies, restaurant management, and many others who manage facilities or work in entry or service positions to which you will need access prior to and during your principal's stay. You will need to request that you be allowed to conduct your own searches without offending in-house security staff. You will need to be able to get permission to go into areas such as kitchens, storage rooms, and staff-only areas. If you don't get permission to do these things, you won't be able to provide complete service to your principal. Gaining good rapport and friendship with every one from the management to the receptionist to the maid can give you a valuable edge. It is often the people in the most basic service positions who can provide you invaluable assistance.

A good negotiator has many skills. These include understanding the process of negotiation, good language skills, listening skills, questioning and information-gathering skills, follow-through, giving effective feedback, dealing with power differences, and anger management.

UNDERSTANDING THE PROCESS OF NEGOTIATION

Negotiations can be as simple as getting permission to park in a no-parking zone while you load your passengers or as complex as agreeing on all of the terms of your employment with your principal or assessing areas of responsibility when more than one security unit is involved. In all cases the approach is the same.

Negotiations have two overlapping levels of interaction. One is the content; the other is the process. The content is what you are negotiating—getting permission to examine the kitchen before your principal comes into the dining area, getting agreement from an in-house security department that you can use their video monitoring equipment, or having your principal agree not to go for a walk in the park with his dog. The process is the style or form of the negotiation session. Process includes things such as where the discussion is held, who speaks first, how decisions are made, and the power difference between the people negotiating. You must be able to control the process of a negotiation in order to be able to control the content.

Controlling the process and the content doesn't mean forcing your wants or opinion on the other side. It means that if you take the responsibility and have the skills to make the negotiation process simple, the end result should be a smoother negotiation session and an agreement that meets the needs of both parties. When you are negotiating, the needs of your principal and the quality of the principal's protection should be the number one issue, not who will look best or have the greatest authority.

COMMUNICATION SKILLS

Communication skills are important. Being the strong silent type may be fine in some situations, but when you need something done, you need good communication skills in order to quickly, clearly, and accurately convey what you need. Depending on who your principal is, this may mean learning another language.

You should strive to choose the right word. This can mean using the jargon used by the person you are talking to. For example, if you want a handgun, depending on the person you are talking to, you might ask for a pistol, heat, sidearm, or piece. With this you might get anything. If you want a specific type of handgun, you might ask for a Smith and Wesson Model 19 with a 3-inch barrel in stainless steel.

You should be exact in your definitions or descriptions when you need personnel, assign time periods, designate areas, plan events and activities, and utilize facilities. If you ask for two men to help you, that is what you will get. However, if you need the men to do certain things and not stand out from your group, you will need to be more specific. For example, you may need two men who are experienced in defensive tactics, who are between 30 and 45 years of age, one of whom has a commercial driver license, and who both need to wear dark gray business suits with a white shirt and neutral tie.

Your voice is part of your communication skills. With practice you can learn how to make it soft, confident, angry, commanding, or any other way you need it to be to match a particular situation. If you have a regional accent, you should take lessons to reduce or eliminate it. Some accents have stereotypes associated with them or may remind a listener of something they dislike or are uncomfortable with. Develop a neutral "television anchor" accent, and your pronunciation will be acceptable anywhere.

LISTENING SKILLS

Half of communication is listening to someone else. If you don't hear the other person, you will never know what he or she thinks, wants, or feels. Good listening skills will greatly enhance your ability to complete a successful negotiation.

There are six things you can do to become a better listener. Start with paying attention to the person who is speaking. Don't let your mind wander; keep it on the words being spoken. Keep an open mind and don't mentally reject or disagree with what you are hearing. Hearing and understanding someone doesn't mean that you must agree with him or her. The more you understand what the person is saying, the better you will be able to respond to his or her facts, logic, or demands.

Use body language. Your own body language affects your ability to listen. Look at the speaker; this helps you pay attention and shows that you are interested in him or her. Maintain a relaxed and open posture to help both you and the speaker relax.

Ask questions when you need the speaker to clarify any point that you don't understand or that you feel you need more information about. Don't interrupt or ask too many questions, however. Occasionally repeat to the speaker points you have heard to show that you are listening and understand what he or she is saying.

Show interest in what you are hearing. Body language and comments will do this. Say things like, "I know that your rules don't generally allow this," or "I can see that you are trying to help me solve this problem."

Don't interrupt the speaker, except to ask him or her to expand on a point. Don't rush the speaker. If you have a limited amount of time, make this clear at the beginning of the negotiation. Don't talk over the speaker. If you want to respond, wait until he or she has finished a point and use body language like holding out a hand to make him or her pause, then reply.

Be aware of the types of people, appearances, traits, and topics that you don't like or feel uncomfortable with. Don't let your bias or prejudice overcome your ability to listen. Ignore the stereotype of the speaker and listen to the words.

QUESTIONING AND INFORMATION-GATHERING SKILLS

Questioning and information-gathering in relation to most simple negotiations generally take place during the negotiation. For more complex negotiations that involve a number of people, issues, facilities, or other matters that you are not familiar with, you will need to gather information before the negotiation begins. How you do this preliminary research will vary depending on your own level of expertise and the issues, people, facilities, or other items you need to research. This is a complex process and a separate issue from the focus of this book.

Gathering information during a negotiation session is generally done by asking questions. You can ask questions to obtain information and facts, to help you understand the other person's point of view, to help break a large issue down into smaller components or steps, to make some information clearer, and to clarify or challenge assumptions.

There are three types of questions: open, closed, and leading. Open questions are usually very broad or general. They are used when you want to get background information or an overview of the person's knowledge or opinion. You might use these when you feel that you are getting resistance from someone and ask, "What kinds of problems have you had in the past with other executive protection agents?" Or when you want to learn about a facility, "What type of security do you have?" These broad questions allow the person to give whatever information, facts, opinions, or interpretations he or she wants. The person can organize the information in any way he or she wants (e.g., chronologically, by incident, in relation to the structure or facility, by comparing and contrasting, or in order of importance). The person who is responding has the power to give you the information in any order, form, and pace that he or she wants.

Open questions are good to give you a broad view of the facts or issues. The speaker, by the way he or she presents the information, will also give you his or her point of view, ranking of importance, and biases. Open questions also give a feeling of power to the speaker that can help in a situation where there is a power imbalance in your favor, professional jealousy, territorial issues, or a possible lack of trust.

Open questions also have a down side. Some people are shy, incapable, or reluctant to freely talk or answer questions. If you ask one of these people an open question, you will probably get only a brief answer that doesn't contain the main points. Other people are unorganized and include information seemingly unrelated to the question, add too much irrelevant background, and take a long time to tell their story. In both of these situations you have to use all your listening skills and sort out what is relevant so you can direct additional questions to get the information you need.

You can use closed questions to focus your information search. Closed questions will limit or restrict the answer, often by requiring only a yes or no answer. For example, "Are there two security guards on duty at the front gate between 3 P.M. and midnight?" Or "Is Ms. Johnson the person I need to talk to about getting a special parking permit?" The other person can just answer yes or can answer no and give you the correct information. You can also use closed questions to get specific information on a generalized statement, for example, "You said the back doors were locked at night. Who is responsible for locking them and what time does this happen?"

Leading questions are ones where you give the information and ask for confirmation. They set out the facts, events, opinions, interpretations, or situations that you assume and want confirmed. For example, "We can park at the rear entrance at 10:30 tonight and your security officer Mr. Waters will be there and unlock the door for us, let us enter, and then relock the door, is that right?" This can be a good way to confirm what you think your agreement is or what the other person has said. Leading questions can backfire if the other person feels that you are putting words into his or her mouth or trying to force your understanding on the negotiation.

NEGOTIATION FOLLOW-THROUGH AND FEEDBACK

Follow-through is making sure you do what you said you would do, don't go places you said you wouldn't go, and in general live up to your terms of the agreement exactly.

You should also make sure that the other party follows through with his or her commitments. If a problem arises where you need to exceed the terms of an agreement, explain the problem (you didn't anticipate this event, you didn't know about this hidden area) and try to get permission before you take the action you need to. If the situation doesn't allow you time to get permission, immediately after you have completed your job, go to the person with whom you negotiated and tell him or her what happened and why you exceeded your end of the agreement. Keeping your word protects your credibility. The need for breaking your agreement shouldn't happen very often because as a good EPP you should have anticipated all contingencies, thoroughly examined the whole scene and known all possible hiding and ambush areas, and known all people who would be in the area.

Giving feedback is important during the negotiation and afterwards. During the negotiation it means letting the person know that you understand his or her position and that you are working toward a solution that will meet the needs of both of you. After a negotiation is over and you have completed your job, it is always a good idea to take a moment and thank the employee, manager, or person who allowed you special privileges. Tell him or her how it made your job easier and your principal safer. If you had any problems or if you have any suggestions that would make your job easier in the future, tell the person and offer to help work on the better system next time. If your principal is a famous entertainer or athlete, you might offer the person a photo or autograph. Make sure you get permission from your principal and get these well in advance so you don't have to bother your principal continually for these. Keep a notebook for yourself and include detailed notes on whom you dealt with, how easy or difficult it was to negotiate, and what problems or good things there were in the location. This will help you the next time you return to that location.

DEALING WITH POWER-STRUCTURE DIFFERENCES

Power is the ability to influence people or events. It is an important aspect of negotiations. A power imbalance occurs when one person has more power than the other. This makes it very difficult to negotiate and come to a mutually agreeable solution. Many times an EPP, because he or she is just an employee, has little power when dealing with outsiders. Other times, because the principal is such a high-profile entertainer, politician, or businessperson, the EPP gains vicarious power.

There are six types of power. Legitimate authority is a type of power that is usually conferred on people such as a president, general, CEO, or the like. This is a very influential type of power. An EPP may have legitimate authority, but it will usually only be in relation to other employees who are lower on the corporate ladder or with other EPPs.

Coercive authority is often used as a backup to legitimate authority. It is power derived from offering rewards or by making threats on behalf of a person who has the capacity to carry out the reward or threat or by a demeanor that convinces others that you have the authority. An EPP may have coercive authority in relation to people he or she is negotiating with for permission to perform searches, special services, or other tasks related to the job of protecting the principal. This power only comes, however, with the prior sanction of the person with the legitimate power.

Expert power comes from education and experience. Your background and reputation may give you power with those whose respect you have gained. It may not be valued by some groups, and without value there is no power. This is often a form of power that EPPs have because of their training and experience. However, some law-enforcement officers, private security agents, or others may not respect the knowledge and experience of all EPPs.

Information power is associated with expert power, but it can also come from other sources. An EPP can have information power because of his or her research and investigation skills. An EPP has information power with the principal because of his or her knowledge of how to protect the principal.

Connection or associated power is derived from those whom you know. This source of power comes from those who convey it to you. Some people feel that it is almost as exciting to deal with an associate of a famous person as to deal directly with the famous person. An EPP who works for a famous entertainer or sports figure will usually be given associated power by the fans. This can make it much easier to negotiate with employees of hotels and other services that you need.

Referent power is personal power or charisma. This usually cannot be developed; you either have it or you don't. It includes such things as style, charm, self-esteem, or being believable. This can be important for an EPP who needs to be able to get along with the principal's family, friends, and business associates.

In every negotiation it is important to be aware of the types and relative strength of the power held by both sides. Using power can be very effective when it is done positively to solicit the other person to help you with what you need. Negative use of power that results in humiliation, fear, or disregard for the other person's feelings or wants usually produces minimum cooperation and little chance of successfully negotiating in the future. Negative use of power won't help your reputation. The EPP community is a small one, and word about uncooperative agents gets around fast.

ANGER MANAGEMENT

Anger on either side reduces the chance of a successful negotiation to near zero. You can stop anger from being triggered or escalating, both in yourself and in the other person.

Anger is an emotion that goes through predictable stages. Anger is always triggered by something such as a comment, action, or situation. The trigger causes an arousal that results in physiological changes in the person's body caused by an increase in adrenaline. This escalates into a crisis phase where the physiological changes reduce the person's ability to think rationally or make good judgments. It is very difficult or impossible to talk to or reason with a person in this phase. Once the crisis phase has been resolved by some action or by a period of time, the recovery phase starts. It is followed by a postcrisis depression before the person's physiological functions return to normal.

To prevent someone else from becoming angry, it is important to watch his or her responses to your comments. If a person appears to take offense or to start to get angry, do something immediately to stop his or her anger from escalating. Two things may work. First, try to find out what bothered him or her. Ask questions so you can show that you are trying to help him or her understand you or your needs and to find out what it is that is making him or her angry. Also show that you are listening to and understanding his or her concerns by giving feedback. This doesn't mean that you are agreeing to anything; it simply means that you are focusing the discussion on dealing with his or her anger for a few moments.

To prevent becoming angry yourself, you have to recognize all your own triggers. Then you have to decide not to allow these triggers to make you angry. Once your anger starts to escalate, your reasoning ability and decision making will be impaired, and you won't be able to do your job.

Sometimes you may have to deal with a person who is already angry because of a person or situation that happened immediately before your meeting. Don't let anyone displace his or her expression of anger at you. Either postpone your meeting by saying something like, "Maybe this isn't a good time to discuss this. Are you free in an hour?" Or take a few minutes and let the person vent his or her anger and get into the recovery phase by talking about what just happened or something neutral.

10

Defensive-Tactics Analysis and Application

The topic of defensive tactics is one that is often misunderstood by those who look toward a career in executive protection. The presumption that the EPP should have guerrilla-warfare–like combat skills is a gross misconception perpetuated in the movies and on television. The topic of defensive tactics is a paradox of sorts. As an EPP, you should possess a high level of proficiency in defensive tactics. In the greater majority of situations, however, if an EPP has done his or her job properly, the need for the use of physical force will be either nonexistent or extremely small. It is not the EPP's purpose or goal to engage an enemy. His or her primary directive is to protect the principal. In most cases this requires that you expeditiously disengage the enemy and remove the principal from the area of danger.

There are three lines of defense: (1) planning and preparation, (2) shielding the principal, and (3) defensive tactics. If the first two are done effectively, there is almost never a need for the third.

PLANNING AND PREPARATION

The first line of defense is planning and preparation. If careful attention has been given to every detail in the preliminary stages, it is unlikely that a physical confrontation will occur. If you study the other chapters of this book diligently and apply what you have learned, it is to be hoped that you will not find the need for a physical confrontation.

SHIELD THE PRINCIPAL

The second line of defense is in shielding your principal from harm. This, along with other elements of planning and procedure, comes under the heading of "hardening the target." The goal is to reduce the principal's level of exposure to possible harm. A word of caution: Your principal may be uncomfortable being referred to as "the target," so refrain from using such terms when speaking to him or her. Your job is to keep your principal safe and to provide a sense of security as well. Even the little things that you do or say will have a direct impact on this goal.

Assuming that the preliminaries such as route planning and advance reconnaissance have been properly done, you will need to properly shield your principal from harm both en route and at location. Our defensive-tactics course divides shielding the principal into three divisions. These divisions are agent proximity, environmental factors, and hardware or armament. These may be used alone or in conjunction with each other.

Agent proximity refers to the EPP's position relative to the principal. This function is almost always tied to environmental factors. This is especially true when you are a sole agent. As a sole agent, you must be ever vigilant in keeping yourself positioned in such a way as to make your principal as inaccessible as possible to those who may seek to do harm. It is the EPP's job to reduce the principal's exposure to any threat. For example, if you are walking along the sidewalk with your principal, next to a building, you may decide to walk slightly behind and to the outside of your principal. In this way you are covering one side of your principal and allowing the building to cover his other side. Assume that you see a stranger approaching from the front coming in the opposite direction. You should first check behind you to be sure that no one is attempting to sneak up from behind. Then, if all is clear behind you, you should move slightly ahead of your principal, placing yourself between the stranger and your principal. As the stranger passes by, you should drop back, always keeping yourself between your principal and the stranger. Once the stranger has passed, you should have moved behind your principal and resumed your original position. In this way you are consistently creating a barrier and shielding your principal from harm.

In a security detail agent proximity is accomplished in large part by use of formations. Depending on the number of agents on the team, the formation will vary. The personal security officer (who is designated by the detail leader) will most likely take his or her position just behind and to the left or right of the principal. He or she is normally positioned only inches from the principal. The others may be in a square, diamond, or other formation grouping. In this way the agents themselves become the shield.

We briefly addressed using environmental factors when discussing shielding by a sole agent. More specifically, this refers to using any object in the environment that can be incorporated into the shielding process, your route plan, or your escape plan. Such objects may include buildings, trees, cars, bushes, lakes or ponds, or any other physical barrier. Form the habit of being aware of these environmental factors at all times. This information is always utilized during route planning and principal positioning (in restaurants, meeting rooms, or other locations) and is an integral part of an overall protection plan. As an EPP, you should always ask yourself, Where might my principal be standing, sitting, or walking? Then analyze your surroundings and see what can be used for cover or concealment during any given scenario. Cover is anything that will protect you, something bulletproof. Concealment is something that blocks vision or that you can hide behind. In your mind, ask, "What if X happens?" Develop as many possibilities as you can imagine that could occur and become dangers to your principal. Then use these possibilities to construct a strategy for shielding your principal.

As well, when considering environmental obstructions, be sure not to box yourself in with the obstructions that you hope will assist you. You do not want to construct a trap for yourself and your principal. Always leave yourself a way out. Constantly ask yourself, If something happened right now, what "hole" could we escape to safety through? It is particularly helpful when you are working as a sole agent to utilize physical barriers. These barriers can double as your inanimate detail partner(s).

Environmental factors can also work against you. An intruder, mugger, or sniper can utilize these same barriers to his or her advantage. Always be aware and on the lookout. Look from ground to rooftop and both near and far. Be leery of anything that looks even remotely out of place or suspicious. As an example, someone crouching on a rooftop with his or her hat turned backwards should trigger caution. Be aware of doors and windows that you will pass that could spring open to reveal an intruder.

The third method of shielding is hardware or armament. This includes such things as bulletproof vests, armored vehicles, and bullet-resistant glass (e.g., in windows or as a shield in front of a podium for speaking engagements). Although these tools are not foolproof, they certainly reduce the level of exposure, thereby reducing the threat.

Remember to remind yourself daily of the old executive protection adage that says, "Today is the day that it could happen." When you become complacent, you place your principal in danger.

DEFENSIVE TACTICS

Although the EPP needs competent defensive skills, you must always remember that it is in both your and your principal's best interest to disengage an enemy and to get the principal to safety. For this reason, executive protection defensive tactics are quite specialized and specific in nature.

If something goes wrong, you may find yourself needing hands-on defensive skills. Situations may range from something as simple as dislodging your principal's hand from the grasp of an overzealous admirer to defending your principal from multiple, armed attackers. It is our belief that the practical application of defensive tactics cannot be taught effectively by any book. Such application requires hands-on training by a competent defensive-tactics instructor who is familiar with the specialized needs of the EPP. Please don't go to your local street-corner karate school and presume that what is being instructed there in any way resembles the specialized tactics needed by the EPP. In most cases that training will not even come close. Most instructors at commercial martial arts schools have no executive protection experience and, in more cases than not, have never been in a real fight. The training at these schools may be great exercise, but it is unrealistic. It does not address the special needs of the EPP. There are places to get the proper training if you do a little looking. At Master's Realm Inc., we often provide training programs, as do a few other organizations that specialize in this type of training. It is of benefit to you to find a competent defensive-tactics instructor with a knowledge of executive protection. Even if you need to travel to attend class, it will be worth the added effort and expense. In a two-week specialized course you will learn more of practical value than you will training under a person without these skills for months or years.

The defensive-tactics system that we use is called the "Six-Zone Safeguard System." The essence of the system is to keep it simple. The system is based on the principle of zoned defense. Where most systems provide a specific defense for a specific attack, the Six-Zone System addresses windows of opportunity or entry. The advantage of a zoned system is this: If you attempted to learn a specific defense for each possible attack, you would need a vast number of applications in order to be prepared for every eventuality. In zoning the specific attack becomes relatively unimportant. What is important is filling the window of opportunity that the attack is passing through to reach its intended target. This system is versatile and simple because you only need to manage each of the six windows of opportunity through which an attack may come.

Although there are some basic guidelines that differentiate defenses against weapons from defenses against unarmed assailants, the basic concepts remain the same in most situations. The zoned format makes defending a much simpler process. Learning to manage six well-defined areas instead of learning hundreds of different defenses for each possible attack is more efficient. In real situations what is simple and direct always works best. There is no time for elaborate fighting techniques or flashy kicks and punches during a street confrontation. Time is of the essence. Defend only to the point that is absolutely necessary and then evacuate your principal. Often assailants will create a disturbance as a distraction in order to get to your principal. While an inept agent is occupied fighting an attacker, another attacker will gain access to the principal. Keep it direct, quick, and simple.

There are some simple formulas for learning competent defensive-tactics procedures. Like anything else, they must be practiced regularly if they are to be effective. The following will outline the Six-Zone System.

THE SIX ZONES

Imagine a line down the front of your body (from head to toe) dividing your body into a left and a right half. Now picture a line across your shoulders and another horizontal line going across at about where your fingertips hang at your side. These are the dividing lines of the six zones of defense. The six zones can also be viewed as windows of opportunity or access. To attack, an intruder must pass through one of these windows. Your job is to fill up the path of entry and prevent the attacker from penetrating your defense with the attack. To stop the attack, you need only close the specific window of entry. This is much simpler than learning a specific defense for every attack.

CONTROL POINTS

There are certain areas of the body that provide an early warning system and give information about an intruder's movement and intentions. If you watch these points, it is easier to predict your attacker's intentions. The knees and elbows are the primary early warning indicators in the Six-Zone System. As an example, the elbow must move in order for a punch to be thrown. Since the elbow moves about one-third the distance of the fist in the same amount of time, it must be traveling about one-third the speed of the fist. As well, if the elbow lifts, you can predict a hook or a punch from an angle. If the elbow moves directly forward, the punch will most likely be a straight punch. If the person attempts to kick, the same principle applies. Simply say that the knee is to the leg as the elbow is to the arm.

There are also points that give the easiest management and redirection of an intruder's attack. The four main control points are the elbows, head, knees, and wrists (in that order).

The management point that you will find useful most frequently is the elbow (figure 10.1). By controlling the elbow, you can virtually control the intruder's entire body movement through the process of redirection. Try it for yourself. Have a partner stand in front of you facing sideways to you. Put your hand around his elbow from underneath and lift the elbow slightly upwards in the direction that he is facing. Now tell him to turn and face you. When he attempts to do so, firmly push his elbow away from you and across his upper abdomen or chest. You will find that this will stop his turn, even if he is bigger and stronger than you. Step forward and push a little further, and you will find that you can turn and redirect him. This is a great tool with which to redirect an attacker away from your principal without being conspicuous or causing a big commotion. These applications, like all others, should be taught hands-on by a qualified instructor.

The head is the second-easiest management point to gain access to (figure 10.2). Even the most obnoxious intruder has the unbending desire to let his body go where his or her head is going. Also, by turning the intruder's head, you place the principal out of

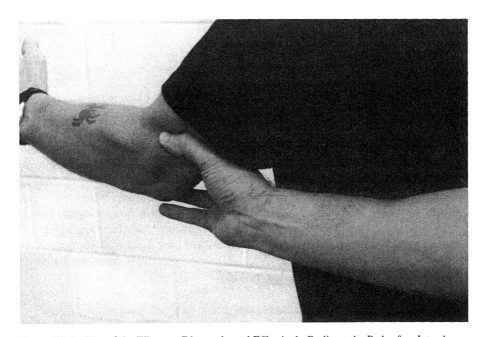

Figure 10.1   Use of the Elbow to Discreetly and Effectively Redirect the Path of an Intruder

Figure 10.2   Use of the Head as a Control Point

the line of the intruder's vision, thereby reducing the threat further. As with all defensive-tactics skills, these techniques should be taught hands-on by a competent and qualified instructor.

An attacker can be slowed down or brought to the ground by disabling his or her knee (figure 10.3). If the attacker cannot walk, he cannot give chase. This will give you ample opportunity to evacuate your principal.

The wrist can be used to inflict massive doses of pain if you know how to do it (figure 10.4). Most people do not like pain and become cooperative when large doses are administered. The problem with this tactic is that you must attain a high level of proficiency in order to be able to apply wrist locks effectively. If you do not have the training and expertise to apply them quickly and effectively, you will find them to be grossly ineffective. Attempting them when you are not properly trained may result in you ending up on the ground in a wrestling match with the intruder. While you are on the ground, you are incapable of protecting your principal further or evacuating him or her from the area. This is to neither your or your principal's benefit. Seek a qualified personal instructor before attempting to use techniques such as these.

DEFENSIVE-TACTICS CONSIDERATIONS

The following are the four major considerations in defensive tactics. You will need to consider and utilize each of these in the planning and execution of every defensive situation.

Figure 10.3   Manipulating or Disabling an Attacker's Knee

1. Evade
2. Confront
3. Management
4. Survival

These considerations can be further broken down into two groups. These groups are (1) course of action, which includes evade and confront, and (2) response, which includes the two levels of management and survival.

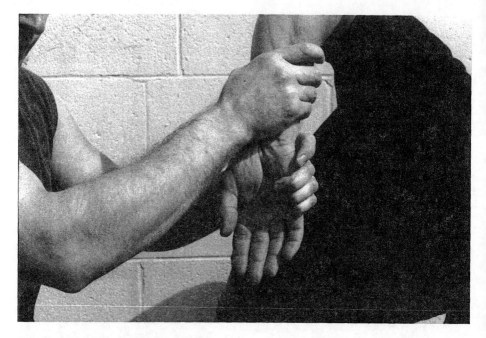

Figure 10.4   Inflicting Pain on an Attacker's Wrist

Evade

It is always best to avoid conflict. Remember that your primary function is to keep your principal safe. An EPP does not try to be "macho." Avoiding danger is not cowardice; it demonstrates professionalism and intelligence. The best defense is not to be in harm's way. Do not tempt fate. The few extra steps needed to avoid a possible threat may save you many steps en route to the emergency room or morgue.

Suppose your principal is confronted by a disgruntled business competitor at a cocktail party. The business competitor is making a scene, accusing your principal of dishonest tactics. The smart thing to do is to gracefully make an excuse that will allow you to get your principal away from the angry competitor. You might say, "Excuse me, sir (or ma'am). I hate to disturb you, but there is an important call that I think you will want to take." You can now step between your principal and the antagonist, guarding your principal's back as you carefully and watchfully escort him or her away. In using this approach you have protected your principal from physical harm and from further embarrassment as well.

In the same situation, suppose that you were to step between your principal and the antagonist and say, "Who do you think you are talking to, big mouth?" The person might then throw a drink on you or your principal, try to strike one of you, or, if he or she has brought a weapon, consider this to be the excuse he or she needs to bring it out. By using this approach you would have subjected your principal to unnecessary risk and embarrassment. You would have failed in the execution of your job. This is not the mark of a professional.

Confront

Confront only as a last resort. Be sure that you have weighed all of the possible consequences of this action in advance. If you do choose to confront, be certain that your skills are up to the task and that your actions will not put your principal in greater danger. As they say, "Never write checks with your mouth that your butt can't cash."

Management

Management is for those instances where no threat to life or limb is perceived. This might include a drunk at a restaurant, an overzealous fan, or a disgruntled employee who may want to embarrass, yell at, or "shake the crap" out of your principal but who has no lethal intentions. In such a situation it would be a gross overreaction to shoot the intruder or break his or her kneecaps. The appropriate course of action is to manage his or her movement by redirecting this person away or restraining him or her. At the same time, remain aware of your surroundings to be sure that there are no other people accompanying this intruder. If you are working with a security detail, one or more detail members should remain with the principal. Whoever removes this person should talk to the person as he or she is being escorted away or restrained. Attempt to calm the person to avoid a bigger scene. You can hand the person off to another detail member who might be able to pacify this person by listening to his or her complaint. Whatever you do, do not release the person until you are sure that he or she is calm and nonaggressive. If the person continues to display aggressiveness, have the person removed to a quiet room or have him or her taken outside while someone on your detail calls the proper authorities. If you are working alone, it is imperative that you do not leave your principal for any longer than is absolutely necessary. Take the person to a door from which your principal is still visible to you. Try to calm the person and then suggest that he or she leave. If the person does not respond to your kind attempts to evict him or her, you may want to ask another guest to contact the authorities. Remember, you are not the police.

Survival

In a survival situation the kid gloves come off. We are now talking about situations where the EPP genuinely feels that his or her life or limb and that of his or her principal is in imminent danger. If this is in fact the case, the EPP must act quickly, decisively, and competently to stop the intruder regardless of the cost to the intruder. In a survival situation your skill level will in great part determine your response. Don't attempt anything that is above your abilities. Evacuate your principal at the first opportunity.

LEVEL OF THREAT AND TYPE OF INTRUDER

There are three levels of threat. These levels are low, medium, and high. Examples of a low-level threat include a nuisance intruder, a heckler at a speaking engagement, a barking dog, a slippery floor, or an admiring but pushy fan. Examples of a midlevel threat include a visibly angry business associate or competitor, a confrontation with someone with political, religious, or social views contrary to those of your principal, someone screaming at your principal or trying to encroach too closely on your principal's immediate territory, verbal threats of physical harm, and the like. Examples of a high-level threat include an intruder trying to manhandle or physically assault your principal, someone attempting to pass through a crowd-control barricade, brandishing or utilization of a weapon, and the threat of explosives or other weapons. If an intruder says that he or she has a weapon, explosive device, or the like, believe him or her and treat it as a high-level threat until you can verify otherwise.

Although an EPP can use these categories as rough outlines to plot a strategy or plan of action, be aware that low- and midlevel threats can easily escalate to high-level threats if they are not properly managed. In the life of an EPP all things are in a constant state of change and flux. The competent EPP can change with whatever the moment requires. Remember that the EPP's job is to reduce the level of threat to an easily manageable level. The EPP's actions should never be such that they antagonize an intruder unnecessarily or in any way elevate the level of the threat. The good EPP leaves his ego behind when he or she goes to work.

There are three types of intruder. They are the annoyance intruder, the assertive intruder, and the aggressive intruder.

An annoyance intruder is normally classified as a low-level threat. This may be an autograph hunter, an admirer, a beggar, or a curious bystander. It is important that an EPP be firm yet polite in dismissing such an intruder. If you were to be rude or pushy in such a situation, the intruder could become agitated. The situation would then escalate.

An assertive intruder is generally a midlevel threat but can sometimes become a high-level threat. The assertive intruder will be pushy and offensive. He or she will often be verbally abusive and physically aggressive. This person tends to be irrational and unreasonable.

An aggressive intruder will do whatever is necessary to gain access to your principal and to achieve the result he or she seeks. He or she will be irrational and give little or no thought to the consequences of his or her actions. This person may rush at your principal. He or she may be attacking with his or her fists or wielding a weapon. This person's sole purpose is to do harm.

Regardless of the level of threat, the best course of action is to evade. As the likelihood of successfully avoiding a confrontation decreases, the likelihood of a confrontation, of course, increases. If this happens, the level of response will shift from management to survival relative to the threat level (low, medium, high). These categories are fluid. They can change from one to another and back again in seconds. As a professional, you must have the ability to quickly analyze the situation and to be able to change your course of action as quickly as the situation changes.

IMPORTANT FUNDAMENTALS

In the Six-Zone System of self-defense it is assumed that in any attack your attacker will be bigger, stronger, and faster and possess some degree of ability. You also need to remember that oftentimes there will be more than one attacker. Bullies are inherent and insecure cowards. They will pick on people over whom they feel they have a physical advantage. This is why they travel in gangs or use weapons to intimidate or harm their victims. For this reason, the Six-Zone System is designed differently than many other systems. This method discourages the use of force against force. If you grapple with a larger, stronger attacker, you are doomed to failure. Our system teaches you how to use the attacker's force and movement against him. This is done through redirection of the attacker's force in combination with moving yourself into a position of greater advantage. Regardless of your previous exposure to this topic, when you are reading this book, we ask you to do only one thing: Take an objective look at the principles involved in a zoned system like the Six-Zone Safeguard System and then ask yourself if they are logical and if they make sense. Aside from the solid reputation of the authors and the developer of this system, the only thing that is important in any system is whether it makes sense. If it is sensible and well organized, it will work.

Management and Redirection

An important principle in managing a larger attacker, retaining your handgun from someone attempting to disarm you, and disarming an armed attacker is the ability to make the aggressor's movement work for you. As previously stated, you should always assume that the attacker will be bigger, stronger, and faster, and you must assume some ability on the attacker's part. This may not always turn out to be entirely so, but in any event you must assume it to be so. In effect, you are hoping for the best but preparing for the worst possible scenario. If you assume that the attacker is smaller, weaker, slower, and stupid, you need no specialized training to manage him or her. Isn't the entire reason you engage in specialized training that of turning the advantage to you?

It is important that you learn to resist any tendency to "control" the attacker. If you attempt to overpower a larger, stronger attacker, you will lose. This is true for both men and women. If you do not use force, the attacker will have no resistance against which to use his or her force. You must learn to utilize the attacker's force and movement to your advantage. Move with the attacker and manage his or her movement. The key to managing the attacker is the redirection of his or her energy and movement. In accomplishing this, you must consider both degree of force and the direction of that force. The degree of force is how strong or aggressive the attacker is. The direction of force is the path or line on which the force is traveling. You can learn to gain a position of safety simply by redirecting the attacker's line of movement relative to the degree of force he or she is using. Although this may sound complex, you will see as we illustrate these principles that it is actually quite simple.

Managing the attacker's movement simply means that you will take the force and movement of the attacker and alter its direction by almost paralleling the movement in such a way as to cause the attacker to miss his or her mark. There is a trick to accomplishing this. You need to realize that all action taken by the aggressor can be of advantage to you. If you learn to see a positive possibility (for you) in every movement your attacker makes, your perception of the events will determine the reality of the outcome. You never want to end up in a force-against-force struggle with an unarmed attacker or for a weapon, especially if your attacker is bigger and stronger than you. If you don't get beat up or shot on purpose, you may be injured by accident in the struggle. Either way, you may be seriously injured or killed.

The key to redirecting an attacker's movement is manipulation of (or steering him or her by) his or her elbow. This is true in self-defense and in both weapon-retention and disarming techniques. The elbow can be used to redirect the position of an attacker or his or her weapon with relative ease.

All techniques in the Six-Zone System are based on two simple principles. First, redirect the attacker's force. Second, step out of the way. We will show you how to use the elbow to redirect the attacker while stepping out of the line of force. Using these principles, you can realign your position (relative to the attacker's) in such a way as to make it difficult for the attacker to continue the attack or to launch a new attack. The worst mistake that you can make is to grapple with a larger attacker or to struggle for a weapon. If you struggle for the gun, an additional danger is created. You may be shot by accident in the struggle. Either way, you lose. You want to avoid any strength-against-strength confrontation.

Making the First Move

It is always to your advantage to make the first move, especially when defending a weapon. Moving first might simply mean that you are careful to take preventive measures by means of your positioning and posturing. It also means that when you are disarming an attacker with a gun, it is too late to react once the trigger is pulled. It becomes essential, therefore, that you make the first move, taking advantage of both your attacker's reaction time and the element of surprise. If you do so, most defenses can be completed in less time than the attacker can react. If you move first and with accuracy, you will succeed. If you wait, you may die. As well, once you commit to a move, you must complete it. If you hesitate or pause in the middle, you will be injured or killed.

Once you have learned the mechanics and the principles, there are three things you need to do to become proficient: Practice, practice, and practice still more. You must do all techniques without hesitation. They must become second nature. This can only be accomplished by practice. Remember as well not to let your skills become stale. If you practice until you have achieved proficiency, and you then neglect to practice and refresh your skills, over time you will lose your edge. If you keep it simple and keep in practice, you will vastly improve your chance of survival.

Key Elements of Weapons Defenses

If your attacker has a handgun or a knife, and you want to manage the weapon, focus your attention on the primary management point, the elbow. The majority of Six-Zone applications revolve around use of the elbow as a tracking point for the attacker's arm and as a manipulation point through which you can redirect the attacker's hand and body movements. You will find that when you are able to redirect the attacker's elbow, you can redirect his entire body (including the weapon hand). This principle is highly effective and reduces and simplifies the number of applications necessary in developing a good defensive-tactics arsenal. We advocate a system that emphasizes learning a few versatile techniques that can be mixed and matched rather than learning many intricate techniques that apply only to one specific attack. In a real situation you may not have the time or might not remember intricate techniques. Remember to keep it simple.

Why the Elbow?

The elbow's movement will give you both an early warning system and directional information. For example, if someone throws a straight punch, his or her fist will travel about a foot compared to about three or four inches traveled by the elbow. This holds true of hooks (circular punches) as well, where the fist makes a bigger circle in the same period of time in which the elbow makes a smaller circle. If the fist is traveling a greater distance in the same period of time as the elbow, it means that the elbow is traveling proportionately slower than the fist. As well, the hand will move respectively in the direction that the elbow moves, giving you an early indicator as to the direction in which the hand is going. In addition to being easier to see, the elbow makes an excellent "handle" by which to redirect movement and offset an attacker's position.

This same principle holds true in disarming and handgun retention. When disarming an attacker, you need to find a secure manipulation point as quickly as possible. If the attacker attempts to move his hand, the elbow will move to a smaller degree and thus be easier to secure. Conversely, once you secure the attacker's elbow, every inch that you redirect the elbow will cause the hand (and weapon) to move a proportionately larger distance and at a faster rate of speed, enabling you to quickly and effectively redirect the muzzle in a safer direction.

Managing the movement of the elbow and stepping out of the line of force, accompanied with a few basic pressure-point attacks or a few wrist and elbow-joint locks, will provide you with a vast array of techniques that you can mix and match. The key is to recognize the threat by reading the early warning signals, and to act quickly and with competence.

WHEN A TECHNIQUE YOU TRY DOESN'T WORK

There is no such thing as the perfect technique. Whether or not any technique will work depends on two criteria, your expertise and that of your opponent. Any instructor who says that he has a technique that will work all of the time against any attacker is either an idiot or a liar. If there were one perfect technique, you could learn only that technique and be prepared for any instance. Due to many factors, including, but not limited to, stress, failure on your part to execute a technique properly, or the ability of the attacker to neutralize that specific technique, you may find yourself in a position where your first technique does not work. If this happens, never try to rehabilitate failure. Don't force or retry the same technique. Abort it and go immediately to another. You do not want to end up in a struggle for dominance with a larger, stronger attacker, especially if he is armed with a gun. Learn to be adaptable.

When you are practicing, have four or five variations and follow-ups to the technique that you are practicing in mind. Randomly, have your partner resist your efforts and react by immediately moving to another application. You must practice them randomly in order to gain the skill of moving between the applications without interruption or hesitation. You can use the "what-if" method to create new scenarios. What if your opponent resists in a certain direction when you try to redirect his move? Let your partner resist and then move instantly to a different application. Then repeat this with other techniques. Be sure to practice in a controlled setting to gain a higher skill level before practicing randomly. Also remember to practice realistically. Once a partner knows what you are planning to do, it is far easier for him or her to foul you up than it would be for someone who has no idea what you are going to do. For example, if you are practicing a technique where you will redirect your partner's elbow to the left, and he or she forces to the right before you even get started, this would be creating an unrealistic scenario. Your real opponent would certainly not move in that way. Training partners need to cooperate by keeping it realistic. Work together to improve both your and your partner's skill level. If you try to foul each other up or tease each other, you will accomplish little.

KEEP A COOL HEAD

If you practice until you are truly confident that you can perform each technique, you will stay calm and relaxed in a real attack situation. If you are relaxed and confident, you will respond with greater skill and accuracy. Remember, you may only get one chance to survive. You don't get a second turn. If you are tense and anxious, you will add to your attacker's anxiety. This will increase the level of the danger. Also, if you are tense, you will be more likely to "telegraph" your intended course of action to your attacker and thereby take away your element of surprise. Take a deep breath, relax, and do it right the first time.

Anger distorts perception. As an EPP, you are a professional. As hard a concept as it might be for some to understand, you can't take anything personally in this business. Even if someone attempts to take your head off with a baseball bat, you cannot take it personally. Such an occurrence is not something to get angry over. It is an opportunity for you to solve a work-related problem. View it in that context, and you will respond more appropriately.

Keep a cool head. Never act from anger. A hothead will not last long as an EPP. It is important that you always have a clear and undistorted perception of what is happening around you and your principal. Train yourself to be objective. Learn to function outside of yourself, even when you are part of the primary circumstance and even if you are wounded by an attacker. Your responses, to a great degree, will be a product of your training. Few people come by it naturally.

If an intruder has done his or her homework, he or she will have a profile on both you (and any other detail members) and your principal. If you are known to be a hothead, this may very well become the means by which he or she misdirects you in order to get to your principal. Don't let other people pull your strings. Leave your ego behind and act as a responsible professional at all times. Don't give a would-be intruder a window of opportunity for entry.

If you are angry, your emotions instead of your intelligence and training will take over. You will slip from the role of protector/parent to one of dependent/juvenile. You are expected to, and should be, competently managing all areas relative to your and your principal's safety. This begins with your ability to manage your own responses.

LIFE AND DEATH

When you are viciously attacked or if a weapon is involved, you must always perceive it to be a life-or-death situation. The best way to stay safe is to avoid ending up in dangerous situations through good planning and preparation. Stay away from people or places that contribute to a lack of safety. Be alert to your surroundings. Be aware of approaching strangers. If you carry a firearm, keep it secure.

Even with good planning and preparation on your part, the unexpected can happen. When a confrontation is unavoidable, keep calm, strike quickly and accurately, and keep it simple to avoid mistakes. Never assume that the attacker is faking. If you are threatened, take it seriously. Don't make the mistake of thinking that the attacker is "only trying to scare you." Even if he is only trying to scare you, you may end up being shot by the knee-jerk reaction of his nervous trigger finger. Once the threat is presented and you have no safe and realistic means of escape, take action. If you hurt your attacker, you may end up in court. Ending up in court beats ending up in the morgue. Once the threat is made, you have been assaulted. Don't wait for the battery. If you believe that you are in imminent danger, act immediately.

11

Auto Search

PREPARATION

Auto search is more difficult in many aspects than building search. There are simply so many places to hide something. What may appear to be a part of the vehicle's electrical system could be something quite different that has been planted there. Also, some people hesitate to look in the deep nooks and crannies and on the chassis. These spots are often greasy, dirty, hot, and hard to access. They provide a perfect opportunity for an intruder to place an explosive device or eavesdropping device.

An auto search is best done with two or three people. Here are some tips for a more effective auto search.

1. *Look:* Look for any sign of tampering.
2. *Clean:* Keep vehicles clean. This is for more than just appearance. It will make it easier to detect fingerprints, dirt smudges, or other signs of tampering.
3. *Debris:* Check for any foreign debris around vehicles. This could be dirt not indigenously found at that location, bits of wire, cigarette butts, paper, or other objects.
4. *Know:* Know how you left the car (especially if you are the driver).
5. *Don't Touch:* Limit touching on the initial inspection. It will be difficult for you to tell who left what marks or fingerprints if you are contributing to the smudges.
6. *Fluids:* Check under the vehicle for leaking fluids.
7. *Chassis:* Utilize a long-handled mirror to check under the vehicle.

THE SEARCH

Although vehicle search and security is always an important consideration, the most dangerous situation arises when any vehicle in question has been in an unsecured area. If this has occurred, it is even more important to conduct a thorough search. Preferably three security detail members should be included in the search. Of these three, two will be observers and assistants. Only one will control any action to be taken.

One helpful hint in detecting an intruder's entry into a vehicle (aside from an intruder alarm system, which can sometimes be circumvented) is simply to place small pieces of tape at inconspicuous spots along door, hood, or trunk openings. If you return to the vehicle and find that the tape seal has been tampered with and restuck or broken, it is an indicator that someone may have attempted to tamper with the vehicle. This is not foolproof, but it can add another layer of protection.

After the initial inspection of the exterior, the detail leader will decide which compartment to open first. We will begin with the trunk.

The first step is to carefully check the groove where the trunk lid meets the auto body. After careful visual inspection, take a piece of stiff paper or a business card and grasp it lightly between two fingers. Place it in the groove and gently run it along the groove. If the card or paper hits a snag, look again for signs of tampering, pry marks, or trip wires. Once this process has been completed, you are ready to open the trunk lid.

To open the trunk, one EPP should put pressure down on the trunk lid to prevent it from suddenly springing open. When the other EPPs are in place, a designated EPP should unlock the trunk. With an EPP on each side and one at the rear, they can slowly begin to open the trunk. The purpose of having EPPs in three different positions is to gain a visual perspective from three different directions. The EPP in charge of lifting the trunk will do so a fraction of an inch at a time. At each increment, all detail members will check. When they all have said "Clear" to the EPP opening the trunk, he or she will open the trunk another notch. The process is repeated until the trunk is fully open. A flashlight is most helpful during this operation.

Again, the visual inspection begins. Before touching anything, look for signs of tampering. If there are no signs of tampering, it is permissible to slowly and carefully begin to remove items from the trunk. Again, ask yourself, If I were attempting to plant a device, where would I put it? Every inch of the trunk must be inspected. Look under the spare tire, around radio speakers or fan enclosures, in tool compartments, and so forth. Look for stripped screws or new scratches. As well, look for wires going to defrosters, speakers, and fans that appear to be unnecessary and trace them. When the trunk is cleared, you can move on to the engine compartment.

It is helpful to have someone on your security detail who is familiar with auto mechanics and auto electrical equipment. Such a person will have an easier time spotting something that is out of place. Prior to opening the hood, inspect as best you can from underneath. You may want to use a "creeper" (a small wheeled dolly often used by mechanics) or mirrors to get a view of the underside of the vehicle. After you have done so, use the same process to open the hood as you did to open the trunk.

One important thing to look for again are wires that appear to go nowhere or that are cleaner, newer, fatter, or thinner or in some way different from the rest. If you see a wire and can't identify its purpose, trace it. As well, look for suspicious objects that may be made to resemble auto parts. If you have kept the engine compartment clean, your search will be easier. Once the engine compartment has been cleared, you are ready to move on to the passenger compartment.

Before entering the passenger compartment, detail members should take positions at different windows in order to observe the interior from various angles. If all appears clear, the go-ahead is given. The detail leader will decide which door to enter through first.

Use the same procedure as you used on the trunk and hood to open the first door. Once inside, check for stripped screws, loose panels, wire fragments, and other items that we mentioned earlier. Look into the seat-belt rollers, and if all appears normal, pull each of them out slowly, looking for foil, wires, or anything that is not normally found there. Check under the seats and floor mats. Check the glove box, ashtrays, and any other storage space in the vehicle's interior.

Next, check to make sure that all of the controls work. Check the emergency brake, car phone, wipers, electric seats, and anything else that you can think of, no matter how insignificant it may seem, right down to the cigarette lighter. Anything that is not working could be a sign that something in the vehicle has been tampered with.

After the vehicle's interior has been cleared, open the other doors, using the same procedure as used with the other doors and hatches. You may then start the vehicle. If you are unable to take it for a short drive (either for security or logistical reasons), at least drive it slightly forward and then backward and put it into all gears. Once you have completed the vehicle search, and the vehicle receives a clean bill of health, it must never be left unattended. If it is left unattended for even a moment, you should repeat the entire process. Again, you must weigh the risk factor of each assignment when undertaking these searches. You are now ready to have your principal on board.

WHAT IF YOU FIND SOMETHING SUSPICIOUS?

Your search should never be done with your principal present. With your principal absent, even if you should find something suspicious, you have not placed your principal in jeopardy. If your principal is not at risk, you have already achieved your main directive.

If you have even the slightest suspicion that the suspicious item may be an explosive device, do not attempt to disarm or remove it. Follow the same procedures that were covered in chapter 4, "General Principles and Procedures," in the section "Suspect a Bomb?" Keep your focus on your job. Your purpose is the protection and comfort of your principal. Take only the emergency actions needed to protect the lives of those in the immediate area. Leave the rest to the bomb squad.

If you suspect an eavesdropping device, you have a few options. You can remove and deactivate the device, you can call in the local authorities, or you can use the device to your principal's benefit. The degree of anonymity desired by your principal and the perceived level of threat will be factors in making this decision. If your principal does not want unnecessary attention drawn to his or her presence, you may choose simply to disable or destroy the device. Be sure to continue searching, though. There may very well be more than one.

If you plan on doing anything other than destroying the device, say nothing aloud that will tip off the people who planted the device that you have found it. Continue on as though you had found nothing. Signal the other detail members that you have found the device but make no verbal announcement or flamboyant gesture (in case someone is watching). Signals for such situations should have been determined in advance. After finishing the search, you might say out loud, "Well, I think it's clean" or something to that effect. Move away and then make your decision about how you will proceed.

If your principal is a political figure or someone who has access to sensitive information, you may want to call in the proper authorities. If your decision is to notify the authorities, do so immediately. Let them do their job and cooperate with them, providing whatever useful information you can.

If your decision is to make use of the device (assuming that it is an eavesdropping device), you must decide what and when is the best counteruse of the device. In all likelihood, you will use it to feed misleading information to those who planted the device. You may give false locations or timetables about your principal's schedule in order to draw them away from your principal. You may also use the dissemination of misleading information to draw them out in order to find out who the intruder/spy is. If you choose to do this, you may want to do it in cooperation with law-enforcement agencies.

12

Building Search

It is important to the safety and well-being of your principal that he or she not be taken into dangerous or compromising situations. Since most meetings are conducted inside buildings, you must know how to properly secure and clear (assure that the room or building is free from danger, eavesdropping devices, and other security threats) any building that you and your principal will occupy. This should be done prior to your principal's arrival at any location whenever possible.

When you are working with a security detail, searches of a building and/or room should be done by the advance personnel prior to the arrival of the principal and his or her party. After the search is completed, secure the room. If you are a single EPP, this job is more difficult. The following are some options to consider that may help you when you are working alone:

1. Speak with building security and find a secured room where your principal can be held while you search the building and/or room.
2. Advance (preinspect) the room yourself and then have building security, or private security that you have obtained, "baby-sit" the room until you return with your principal.
3. Have the driver of your principal's vehicle continue on while you advance and search the building or room. Securely lock the room and then signal the driver to bring in your principal. Meet your principal at the car and escort him or her to the building or room. If possible, have the principal's vehicle pull up where you can keep the area your principal will occupy in sight. In this way you will be able, to some extent, to see if anyone attempts to enter or exit.

When you are doing a building search, search the building room by room and in levels. Include searching above drop ceilings when they are present by lifting the ceiling tiles from the rails they sit in and inspecting with a bright flashlight. You should also feel carpeting to see if there is anything lying underneath. For example, you may elect to start at ceiling level and work your way down. Each level to be examined should be about 1 to 2 feet in depth. When you finish one level, move on to the next until you reach floor level. If there is a basement underneath or an attic above, it is advisable to search these areas in the same manner.

You will primarily be searching for three things: intruders, explosive devices, and eavesdropping devices. Intruders, of course, will be the easiest to find because of size.

Explosive and eavesdropping devices are often more difficult. If you find one thing, don't stop looking; there may be more. Always complete your search.

When you are looking for intruders, check closets and showers, under beds, behind curtains, and in cabinets large enough to house even the smallest midget. You might ask yourself, "If I were a kid, what great places would I find to hide?" Sometimes, as adults, we overlook the obvious.

What do you do when you find something? If it is an intruder, what you do will largely depend on his or her behavior (see the chapter on defensive tactics). Again, remember that you are not the police. Do not put your hands on this person unless you are physically threatened and must defend yourself, or unless the laws of that state or municipality permit you to do so. Some states allow you to subdue an intruder under certain circumstances; others demand that you allow the intruder to escape if he or she attempts to. Get an accurate and detailed description, tag number of his or her car, and any other information that may help in identifying the intruder. Call the authorities as soon as possible so they can begin an investigation and so there is a formal record of the intrusion.

If you find an eavesdropping device, you may want to disable it, trace it, or use it to feed other information than that expected to the eavesdropper. Exit the room quietly and advise your principal. Weigh your options before making a decision. If it is audio eavesdropping equipment that you discover, you will have some time to make a choice about what to do. If it is video eavesdropping equipment, and if it is active at the time you discover it, the perpetrators will probably know that you have found the device. If they are to be caught, you will need to act quickly. Call the authorities (911 if available) and then attempt to trace wires (if the device is hardwired) or watch outside for anyone carrying electronic equipment from nearby rooms or buildings. It is important that you call the authorities first. If you are subsequently involved in an altercation with the spies, you may need this documentation to show that you were attempting to proceed in accordance with the law. Otherwise, if you are attacked by the spies, they could very well say that you attacked them first and for no reason. Cover your back.

EXPLOSIVE DEVICES

There are many different types of explosive devices, ranging from simple pipe bombs to extremely sophisticated devices. They are all extremely dangerous. Unless by some remote chance you are highly trained in this field, you do not have the skill to handle such devices. Even if you do have the skills needed, it is not your job to do so. Your job is the protection of your principal. Just as you are not the police, you are not the bomb squad. The police bomb squad should handle any such device. As the Amityville Horror House said to the homeowners, "Get out!"

Explosive devices are more effective when they are placed in the immediate vicinity of the intended victim. As an EPP, ask yourself, If I were planting a bomb, where would I expect the target to be and how could I best place the device(s)? The answer may depend in part on what type of device is used. Explosive devices may be timed, have a release or trigger-type detonator, be pressure activated, or be remote controlled. You can reduce the possibilities as to which might be more practical for an intruder to use by careful planning and preparation of your principal's trip.

If you follow our prescription for not being routine or having a fixed schedule, it reduces the opportunity for a timed device. Your scheduled meeting times and places should be held in strict confidence. Only those with a need to know should know times and locations. It is often harder to keep the place a secret than it is the time. For example, if you are renting a hotel room or conference room, more people with low-level security clearance may be privy to that information than those who will know the time of the meeting. If the time of the meeting is unknown, it is unlikely that a timed device would be used. As well, in high-risk assignments it is advisable to obtain multiple locations. You can then advise the parties that are to be present at the last possible moment which location they will need to meet at. If the intended victim is your principal, then the attacker will want to be sure that the principal is present at the time of detonation. Pressure-activated devices do not discriminate. Unless the intended victim is present, the device cannot accomplish the goal. During your search, think to yourself, "Where will my principal be sitting or standing? Is there any object that he or she will be the primary person picking up or handling, such as a package, clipboard, or box?" Scrutinize these carefully in your search. The same applies to trigger-type devices. Check areas to which your principal may have sole access for spring-loaded detonators, electronic detonators, or trip wires. Closet doors, drawers, cameras, recorders, and briefcases make excellent candidates as hiding places.

The possibility of remote detonation can be minimized by keeping shades pulled, by keeping location a secret, and through the use of high-tech scanning devices. Keep in mind as well that detonation methods can be used in combination. It is possible, for instance, to arm a pressure-sensitive explosive remotely so that it cannot detonate prematurely. Your initial room search is your best defense against all of these methods.

ELECTRONIC EAVESDROPPING DEVICES

The same principles for search and prevention that apply to explosives apply to electronic bugging devices. By maintaining confidentiality and limiting access to secured areas, you can minimize the possibility for electronic eavesdropping.

Unlike explosives, modern advances in electronics have made it possible to eavesdrop at a distance. Almost anyone can now plant a small listening device. They are available at many electronics stores. Fortunately, these advantages are a double-edged sword. They make available to you the use of high-tech scanning devices that can help to locate room bugs. To combat the use of long-range listening devices, jammers are available and can be purchased from certain specialty stores. To some degree, radios and televisions running during "quiet" conversation can impair the use of long-range devices. We recommend that you read literature on such devices, visit electronics specialty stores, and take any courses or seminars that you can on this subject given by experts in this very specialized field.

During your search, look for small wires that seem to lead nowhere. Look in any object that could have a hollow interior and be hiding a small transmitter or recorder.

Check in phones, in light fixtures, under chairs and tables, behind paintings, and so on. A good practice is to pretend that you are hiding a bug and to see how many places there are that you might put one. Then, assume these to be the places that someone else might place a bug.

If any intruder or device is found, move your meeting or stay to another room if possible. Security has been breached, and there is no point in taking chances. You must now begin again by searching the new room(s).

13

Firearms

A firearm is an important tool for the protection of your principal. To carry and use a firearm, you must follow all the safety rules and laws for firearm use. In addition, you must carefully choose the best firearm for yourself and the situations you will encounter, carry it in the most practical way, and use it with precision and emotional control.

SAFETY

Safety is always the first consideration of firearm possession and use. There are many safety rules for firearms, which are listed in books and provided in courses. No matter how much experience you have or how proficient a shooter you are, you always need to follow the *two primary* firearms safety rules:

1. Control the direction of the muzzle and never point a firearm at anything you do not intend to shoot.
2. Keep your finger off the trigger until you are ready to shoot.

These primary safety rules apply when you are handling, cleaning, loading, unloading, holstering, or moving a firearm and when you are putting one into or removing one from a case. The primary safety rules apply at a shooting range, in your home, in a vehicle, and everywhere you are when you have a firearm.

Take shooting courses. Take every course you can because you will always be able to learn something new about firearms, ammunition, safety, and how to shoot. There are courses on combat shooting, decision making and shooting (shoot/don't shoot situations), speed shooting, and much more. These are often expensive and require time and travel, but they will be worth it if you ever get into a situation that requires you to shoot to defend your principal. Get the best equipment you can. Everything you use should be the best you can get, including guns, ammunition, and other equipment such as holsters, magazine or speed-loader pouches, cleaning supplies, and gun cases. Take good care of all your equipment by keeping it clean and taking firearms to qualified gunsmiths for any repair or modifications. Good equipment will help ensure that your firearms and ammunition don't drop on the floor when you move or sit, and don't get damaged from bumps, heat, or rain.

Never allow anyone else access to your firearms, ammunition, or equipment. You don't want anyone to damage your equipment, and you don't want to be liable for any harm another person does with it.

Don't use alcohol or drugs when you are in possession of or carrying a firearm. Of course you won't be consuming alcohol while you are responsible for your principal, but also abstain when you are off duty and armed. Drugs, even prescription and over-the-counter ones, can impair your ability to make quick, accurate decisions, perform fine body movements (like drawing and shooting), and accurately and clearly see your front sight. Even drugs that don't have warnings like "avoid use of heavy equipment" may still impair your ability to use a handgun safely.

LEGALITIES

There are many federal and state laws that regulate the possession and use of firearms. It is your responsibility to know and obey all that apply to you. Look for books that set out all the federal law and state laws. Some are listed at the end of this chapter.

You will need to have a license or permit to carry a concealed firearm if such is permitted in your state. Generally the concealed-carry license or permit that is allowed for civilian carry won't be valid for use for a professional such as an EPP. The type of firearm-carry license or permit that an EPP requires may be found under the laws regulating security guards or private investigators. The licensing requirements may require extensive training, a form of "apprenticeship," being an employee of a licensed agency, and obtaining a security guard or private investigator license prior to being able to obtain a license or permit to carry a firearm for your work as an EPP. Such a license may not be valid in other states, or may only be valid in other states if you obtain some prior authorization from the other state. You must check with each state you intend to enter.

Some states may limit the type of firearm or ammunition that may be carried and used by a person with this special carry license or permit. In Florida, for example, one class of license holders may only carry a .38 or .357 caliber revolver with factory .38 caliber ammunition only, and the other class may only carry a .38 or .357 caliber revolver with .38 caliber ammunition, or a .380 or 9 mm semiautomatic. These license holders in Florida are also restricted to only two firearms. Violation of the provisions regarding the firearms license can result in the revocation of the license, so it is very important that you know the law in your state and follow it.

LIABILITIES

If you draw your firearm against someone or shoot someone, you may be liable for a crime or a civil action. You should learn as much as possible about criminal and civil liability and the justifiable use of deadly force. You can learn this by reading and taking courses. (See the books listed at the end of this chapter.)

If you are ever involved in a gun or shooting incident, it is important that you keep a record of what happened so you will be able to accurately recall this if you are involved in a criminal or civil action. As soon as the shooting is over, and when it is safe, quickly write down the following:

1. The exact events, words, behaviors, weapons present, and the like that made you believe that you or your principal was in immediate danger
2. What these made you feel about your own imminent safety
3. Why you didn't or were unable to escape or evade the danger
4. What you did (if anything) to avoid, prevent, or deescalate the danger
5. How the attack started and progressed
6. Exactly what you did to protect your principal and yourself
7. How the incident ended

When you make these notes, stick to the facts, that is, what you saw, heard, smelled, physically felt, and did. You can add your interpretations about these facts, for example, "I saw him bring the muzzle of the shotgun up toward my principal, and I believed he was in imminent danger of being killed." Don't write down what you think the attacker was thinking or what you think his motivation was; just stick to the facts. For example, you can write, "He yelled, 'I'm going to kill you.'" Don't write, "He wanted to kill me."

Make a list of all witnesses at the scene and get their phone numbers. As soon as the police arrive, many potential witnesses will melt away and you will never find them again, so get their names right away. If you are in a public place, take down the license-plate numbers of all the cars in the area. Some of the owners may be witnesses to what happened. Likewise, make a list of businesses that overlook the scene.

Don't talk to anyone about what happened until you have an attorney with you. The stress and adrenaline of a life-threatening encounter will reduce your ability to perceive the facts as accurately as you need to. Tell the police that you won't make any statements until you have your attorney present, and then keep quiet. Once your attorney advises you to talk to the police, be as cooperative as you can. Never lie to the police. Never tamper with evidence at the scene. This is illegal, will cause you endless trouble, and will probably land you in jail.

A shooting will never solve a problem; it will be the start of your problems. If you are arrested or detained, you won't be able to protect your principal. If you are convicted, you won't be able to practice your profession. Even if you are charged but later found innocent, you will have spent a great deal of time, money, and heartache and will have been unable to practice your profession while you were tied up with legal hassles.

HOW HANDGUNS WORK

Handguns are basically very simple machines. The action loads a cartridge into the chamber. When you pull the trigger, the hammer hits the firing pin and forces it against the primer in the cartridge. The primer explodes and sends a spark through the flash hole. The spark ignites the powder, which burns very rapidly, creating gases that expand and fill the space in the cartridge case. The expanding gases push the bullet out of the case and down the bore. When the gases come out of the end of the muzzle, they create the noise of the gunshot.

TYPES OF HANDGUNS

There are two basic types of handguns—revolvers and semiautomatic pistols. Revolvers are all basically similar. They have a cylinder that contains the ammunition and rotates or revolves to align a chamber containing a cartridge between the firing pin and the barrel. There are a great many different designs of semiautomatic pistols. Generally they have in common a magazine of ammunition in the grip and a slide over the barrel. When the pistol is fired, the slide is forced back and it ejects the empty case; then, as it moves forward, it picks up a new cartridge from the magazine and pushes it into the chamber. This happens on each trigger pull.

PARTS OF A HANDGUN

Handguns have four basic parts—a barrel, action, grip, and frame. The barrel is the tube through which the bullet passes. The action includes the moving parts of a handgun. The action does a number of things, including loading and firing the cartridges and ejecting the empty cases. The grip is the handle or part you hold. The frame is the body of the handgun that connects or holds all the parts together.

Barrel

Handgun barrels are thick-walled tubes made of hardened steel. Barrels come in many different lengths, the most popular for EPP work being from 2 to 6 inches long. A bullet shot from a longer barrel is more accurate and will travel faster and go farther because the powder has more time (i.e., distance) to be completely burned, causing greater pressure to expel the bullet. Short barrels are popular because they can be more easily carried and result in lighter handguns for shooting comfort.

The hole inside the barrel is the bore. There are spiral grooves, called rifling, cut into the bore. These grooves have a gradual twist. The twist is measured in the number of inches in length it takes for a spiral to make a 360-degree rotation inside the bore. The area between the grooves is called a land. The inside of the bore, therefore, is made of alternating lands and grooves. Rifling causes the bullet to rotate as it moves along the barrel. This rotation causes the bullet to spin, creating more stable flight through the air. The result is more accurate and longer shots.

The chamber is the part of the handgun that holds the cartridge during detonation. In a semiautomatic pistol the chamber is a very thin area cut into the breech end of the bore. The rifling starts at the end of the chamber and goes to the muzzle. In a revolver there are a number of chambers in the cylinder. There can be up to nine, but most commonly there are five or six chambers.

Because the diameter of the chamber is slightly larger than the diameter of the bore, there is at its end a slight ridge that prevents a cartridge from going any deeper into the barrel or cylinder. This prevents the loading of a case that is of the wrong (but similar) caliber.

Action

The action is a system of moving parts that loads, fires, and ejects a cartridge. It includes the trigger, hammer, firing pin, and a number of small working parts. There are two types of actions: single action and double action. A single action does only one (a single) movement: when the trigger is pulled, the hammer falls forward. To fire a single-action handgun, you must manually cock or pull the hammer back before you pull the trigger. A double action does two things: as you pull the trigger, the hammer cocks and then falls forward.

The trigger is the lever that you pull to fire the handgun. Each make and model of handgun has its own trigger characteristics, including the weight of the trigger pull, the distance the trigger moves, the amount of "play" in the trigger movement before the trigger movement commences, the trigger release characteristics, and the shape and surface of the trigger. When you get a new handgun, test the trigger to discover how each of these characteristics feels. A qualified gunsmith can work on your trigger to make the trigger pull smoother and lighter if you need this. Pulling the trigger causes the hammer to fall.

The hammer is the part that forces the firing pin forward against the cartridge, resulting in the gun firing. There are many styles of hammers in different models of handguns. Often the hammer has a flat front end, but some hammers have the firing pin on the front end. Many hammers have a spur on the back end to allow you to use your thumb to cock the hammer so you can fire the handgun single-action. Those that do not have a spur are called spurless or are sometimes referred to as hammerless (although this is a misnomer). If there is no hammer spur on a revolver, it will only fire double-action, since you cannot manually cock the hammer to fire it single-action. Some revolvers have the frame built up to cover the hammer's arch of movement, either open or closed at the top. These are called shrouded hammers. Semiautomatic pistols may have a hammer with a spur or have an internal hammer in the slide.

The firing pin is a thin rod that is located in the frame, in the slide, or on the end of the hammer. It is the part that hits the primer to cause the cartridge to fire.

Revolvers are made as single-action or double-action handguns. Single-action revolvers are the "cowboy six-shooters" and are not suitable for self-defense or EPP work because they are slow to load, fire, and unload. If a double-action revolver has a hammer spur, you can fire it double-action by just pulling the trigger, or, if you cock the hammer with your thumb, you can fire it single-action. Revolvers that don't have a hammer spur can only be fired double-action (because you can't cock the hammer). When the hammer comes back, either manually or with the trigger pull, it rotates the cylinder to bring the next chamber into line between the firing pin and barrel to be fired.

Semiautomatic pistols can be single-action or double-action. Single-action pistols can only be fired single-action. When the pistol is loaded (if it has a hammer, the hammer must be cocked), it is ready to fire. It is important to keep the external safety on until you are ready to fire (if the pistol has an external safety). Every time you pull the trigger, the gun will fire in a single-action mode because the slide will cock the hammer as it comes back to eject the empty case.

Double-action semiautomatic pistols can be double-action only or first-shot double-action. Double-action-only pistols are just that; every shot is double-action. Most double-action pistols, however, allow you to make the first shot the only double-action trigger pull. The rest of the shots are single-action. When you load a double-action pistol, releasing the slide puts a cartridge into the chamber and leaves the hammer cocked. You must decock the hammer to make it double-action. With some pistols you must do this manually by holding the hammer back with your thumb, carefully pulling back to release the pressure on the trigger, removing your finger from the trigger, and slowly lowering the hammer to the down position. Most double-action pistols have a decocking lever that allows you to push the decocking lever down. The hammer will then fall into a double-action position without firing the pistol. Some decocking levers will spring back to their original position; others act as a manual safety in the down position. You will have to release the safety before firing the pistol.

Grip

The grip is the part of the handgun that you hold when firing. Grips vary in size and shape depending on the model of the handgun. On revolvers it is easy to replace the grip, but on semiautomatics, only the side plates can be changed.

Frame

The frame is the body of the handgun. The design of the frame is important since it determines the overall size of the firearm. Legally the frame is the firearm. It has the serial number stamped on it and possession of a handgun frame is possession of a handgun.

Safeties

Revolvers don't have external safety mechanisms. Modern revolvers do, however, have internal safety devices that prevent them from firing if they are dropped. These are usually either a hammer block, a device that sits between the hammer and the firing pin when the hammer is down, or a transfer bar, which is a device that leaves a gap between the hammer and the firing pin until the revolver is fired.

Semiautomatic pistols have both external and internal safety devices. The external devices vary from one model to the next. The most common external safety is a safety lever located at the rear of the slide. It is either pushed up or down to be on safe. Sometimes the safety is incorporated into the decocking lever. Other types of safeties are the grip safety, the trigger safety, and a safety located in the magazine well that prevents the pistol from being fired if there is no magazine. Read the manual for your pistol to find out what types of safeties are on your pistol.

Sights

Handguns have two sights, a front sight and a rear sight. The front sight has the appearance of a post when viewed from the back of the gun. The rear sight has a square notch in it. The rear sight may be a separate unit fixed onto the rear of the barrel or slide, or it may be a "groove" cut into the rear top strap of a revolver frame.

LOADING AND UNLOADING

Safely loading and unloading a handgun is an important skill. This book will cover only the basic safe way to load and unload. There are methods for speed reloading that are often taught in more advanced shooting courses or books.

Revolvers

To load an empty revolver, follow these steps: (1) Hold the revolver in your right hand. Put your left hand under the trigger guard so your fingers reach up to the cylinder. Press the cylinder release latch with your right thumb and, at the same time, push the cylinder out with the fingers of your left hand. (2) Keeping your right hand on the grip *and your finger off the trigger,* point the revolver straight down. The cylinder will be open to the left side of the revolver. Pick up cartridges with your left hand and drop them into the chambers. If you have the revolver pointed straight down, the cartridges should fall right into the chambers. If the revolver is at an angle, you may have to push them completely in with your finger. Load one cartridge into each chamber. (3) Keeping your finger outside the trigger guard, raise the revolver until the barrel is about parallel to the ground. Touch the bottom of the trigger guard lightly to your left hand, place your left fingers around the right side of the revolver, and push the cylinder closed with your left thumb. Grip the cylinder between your left thumb and fingers and rotate it to make sure it is locked into place (you will hear a click and it won't rotate). The revolver is now loaded.

To unload a revolver or to remove the empty cases after firing, follow these steps: (1) Hold the grip in your right hand and *keep your finger outside the trigger guard.* Put your left hand under the trigger guard so your fingers reach up to the cylinder. Press the cylinder release latch with your right thumb and, at the same time, push the cylinder out with the fingers of your left hand. (2) Let your two middle fingers follow the cylinder through the opening in the frame while you keep your left index finger on the barrel and your left little finger on the hammer. Let the revolver frame lie in your left hand for support. Remove your right hand from the grip. (3) Turn the muzzle of the revolver straight up. Put the tip of your left thumb on the top of the ejector rod and push it down. This will push the star and remove the cases from the cylinders. You may have to pump the ejector rod a few times if any of the cases are stuck. If a case gets caught under the star or against the grip, use your right-hand fingers to pull it free. (4) Reload the revolver or close it empty for transport or storage.

It is important that you always let the empty cases fall to the ground when you empty your revolver. You can pick them up later at the end of your range session. Practicing this will make sure that you never waste time trying to hold empty cases at a time when you should be reloading quickly in a shooting competition or in a self-defense situation.

Semiautomatics

To load a semiautomatic handgun, follow these steps: (1) Load the magazine with ammunition. (2) Hold the handgun in your shooting hand (right hand for most people) keeping the muzzle pointed in a safe direction and your finger out of the trigger guard. (3) Using your other hand, insert the loaded magazine into the magazine well in the frame. Push it in with your palm until it clicks into place. (4) If the slide is locked open, press the slide release. If the slide is closed, grip the slide release with your support hand and pull it fully open, then release it so the slide freely closes. Do not hold the slide and ease it closed because it may jam or not fully close. *Make sure your finger is not on the trigger during loading.* (5) If there is a safety, put it on. Decock the hammer, if there is a decocker lever.

To unload a semiautomatic handgun: (1) *Take your finger off the trigger and out of the trigger guard* and keep the muzzle pointed in a safe direction. Keep the handgun in your shooting hand. (2) Press the magazine release and let the magazine fall to the ground. (3) Use your support hand and quickly pull the slide open to eject the round that is in the chamber. You may need to do this a few times or to slightly turn the gun to let the round drop out onto the ground. (4) Look at the chamber to make sure that there isn't a round in it. (5) Leave the slide locked open or press the slide release to close the slide.

POSSIBLE PROBLEMS

There are several mechanical and functional problems that may happen to handguns. New shooters sometimes don't pull the trigger all the way back if they are shooting fast. The cylinder rotates partially and the hammer comes down easy. This is called roll-by. The new shooter may think that this is a misfire, but all that has happened is that the hammer was never fully cocked, so the revolver didn't fire. However, the cylinder moved out of alignment and should be locked with the support hand before firing. Depending on which direction the shooter locks the cylinder, a live cartridge may be skipped.

If the cylinder becomes out of alignment, the cartridge will blow out to either side, causing a buildup of lead shavings between the cylinder and the forcing cone. A large buildup will prevent the cylinder from rotating.

If the ejector rod is loose, the cylinder won't close, or pressure will be put on the pin at the front of the ejector rod and it will freeze up. If this happens, put pressure on the cylinder release latch and hit the cylinder open.

If a semiautomatic pistol doesn't go off, it may be a misfire or no cartridge in the chamber. Tap and rack. Tap and rack means hit the bottom of the magazine with your left hand to make sure it is securely in the pistol (tap), and pull the slide back and let it go (rack), ejecting the cartridge or case in the chamber and loading a new cartridge.

If the ejected case doesn't fully eject and gets caught in the ejection port as the slide comes forward, it will stick out and look like a stovepipe. If this happens, put your support hand on top of the barrel near the front sight and run your hand quickly along the top of the barrel back toward your shoulder. It will catch the round or case and knock it out. Then tap and rack, even if you eject a cartridge.

Sometimes a second cartridge moves up during loading and causes a jam called a double feed. To clear this, lock the slide back. Dump the magazine. Rack the slide a number of times. Put in a new magazine. If you only have one magazine, don't drop it on the ground; pull it out and put it in your belt or a pocket while you rack the slide, then replace it.

AMMUNITION

Parts of a Cartridge

A cartridge or round of ammunition has four parts: a case, primer, powder, and bullet. The case is the container that holds the other parts. It is a metal tube that is closed at one end called the case head. The caliber of the round is stamped into the case head. It has a rim around the closed end. There are two types of ammunition: center-fire and rim-fire. In center-fire ammunition the case head has a circular indentation in the center of the head with a hole in the center of the indentation. This is the primer pocket and flash hole. In a rim-fire case the case head is flat. The descriptions in this book will refer to center-fire ammunition.

The primer is an explosive device that sits in the case head. In center-fire ammunition it sits in the primer pocket and is flush with the case head. In rim-fire ammunition a priming compound is located inside the rim of the case.

Modern ammunition uses smokeless powder. This is located inside the case. The amount and type of powder vary according to the caliber, bullet weight, and manufacturer. When you buy ammunition, the box does not give you any information on the powder charge. If you hand-load your own ammunition, you can choose from a variety of powder types and will select the amount to use from loading manuals. Some ammunition has a larger powder charge. This is called +P or ++P ammunition. This will be printed on the box and stamped on the case head. It can only be used in handguns that are manufactured to withstand the additional pressures created by firing this ammunition.

The bullet is the projectile. Calling a cartridge a bullet is a misnomer, since the term "bullet" only refers to the projectile, not the whole cartridge. Bullets are usually made of lead, but some are now made of bismuth. They can also be lead covered by a full or partial metal layer called a jacket.

Bullets come in various calibers to match the handgun they are to be used in. They also come in a variety of weights and shapes. The bullet weight affects the velocity of the bullet and the amount of recoil you feel when you shoot the handgun. Ammunition has the bullet weight and type printed on the box, for example, 125 gr JHP.

Bullet shapes include wadcutter (WC), a flat lead plug that has its front edge level with the case end. Wadcutters are used mainly in revolvers, since they won't feed into most semiautomatic pistols. They are used for target shooting on paper targets since they make a clean-edged, circular hole that is easy to score. The semiwadcutter (SWC) is a lead bullet with a flat-ended cone protrusion and a small flat shoulder. Semiwad-cutters are used for target shooting on paper targets since they make a clean-edged, circular hole that is easy to score. The cone allows them to feed in semiautomatic pistols. Round-nose (RN) bullets are usually lead bullets that have a rounded front end without any shoulder. They are generally used for target practice. The holes in paper targets from round-nose bullets have radial tears and are not the best for competition with a bull's-eye target. Ball or full metal jacket (FMJ) bullets are round-nose bullets that are covered with a metal jacket. These are often used for target practice and are preferred by some shooters because they don't leave lead residue in the barrel that lead bullets do. Hollow-point (HP, JHP) bullets are blunt-end round-nose bullets that have a hole in the front end. When these bullets hit fluid material, they expand outward. This is called mushrooming since the expanded bullet shape looks similar to a mushroom shape. These bullets are used as self-defense ammunition since they expand to almost twice their caliber size, resulting in a larger hole and more damage to the person hit. Hollow-point bullets can be lead or jacketed. Some, named Hydroshock®, have a post in the center of the hole. There are many types of hollow-point bullets. Select one that feeds well in your handgun and has a bullet weight that will meet your defensive needs.

Ammunition Safety

Always make sure you have the correct caliber of ammunition for your handgun. There are three things you should check: (1) caliber printed on the box; (2) caliber stamped into the case head; and (3) caliber stamped on the barrel of the handgun. If these three don't match exactly, don't use the ammunition in your gun. Just because a cartridge fits in the chamber of a handgun doesn't mean that it is safe to shoot. The caliber must be the exact one for the handgun.

There are some calibers that are similar. For example, if you have a .22 Magnum handgun, .22 Long Rifle ammunition won't work. You must make sure you get .22

Magnum ammunition. Likewise, .380 is not the same as .38 caliber ammunition. In .38 caliber there are three different types of ammunition: .38, .38 Special, and .38 Super. Check the stamp on the barrel of your handgun and ask for ammunition that is exactly in that caliber.

Of course, as with most things, there are some exceptions. There are some calibers of ammunition that can be used in handguns of similar caliber. For .22 caliber, which come in Short, Long, and Long Rifle, the only difference in the three types is the length of the case. A .22 Long Rifle handgun has a chamber that is long enough for the .22 Long Rifle, which is the longest of the three types. You can use a .22 Long and .22 Short in this handgun because they are the same caliber (diameter) and the length of the case is less than the length of the chamber, which allows them to fit into the chamber. The handgun will shoot the ammunition even though it doesn't go to the end of the chamber, since it is held in place by the rim on the head of the case. Likewise, you can use .22 Short in a .22 Long handgun. However, you cannot use a .22 Long Rifle in a handgun chambered for a .22 Long or .22 Short. The ridge at the front of the chamber won't allow the cartridge to be fully seated, and the head of the case will project out beyond the chamber. This won't let the action close and won't allow the round to be fired.

This situation is similar for .38 Special and .357 Magnum ammunition. Despite the difference in numbers, these are the same diameter, but a .357 Magnum case is longer than a .38 Special case. Therefore, you can shoot .38 Special ammunition in a .357 Magnum handgun, but not vice versa because .357 Magnum ammunition is too long to fit into a .38 Special chamber. Most people use .38 Special ammunition in their .357 Magnum handguns when they practice because it is less expensive. The same principle allows you to use both .44 Magnum and .44 Special ammunition in a .44 Magnum handgun, but not vice versa. There are other calibers with similar correlations, so ask when you are buying a new handgun if this is the case with the one you are considering.

Care of Ammunition

Keep ammunition clean. If any oil residue from your handgun gets on the ammunition, wipe it with a dry clean cloth. Keep ammunition away from solvent and penetrating oils. These may seep in around the primer and deactivate it. This will make your ammunition incapable of firing and may put you in a dangerous position if you rely on it for self-defense. If your ammunition gets wet in the rain, from sweat, or from any other source of water, dry it thoroughly and don't put it back into a damp box.

Storage of Ammunition

Always store ammunition in a place where it is not accessible to children or careless adults. It is best to store ammunition in the box it came in. Then you will always know what you have. The box will also help keep dust, dirt, and moisture off the ammunition. Keep ammunition in a cool, dry location. Surplus military ammunition boxes are good for storage. They are fairly watertight. They also may prevent a dangerous explosion of ammunition in a home fire (reported cases indicate that the ammunition was destroyed but did not escape the box).

Ammunition Problems

Most ammunition problems come from poorly made hand-loaded ammunition. Four ammunition problems you may encounter are a high primer, no powder charge, a double powder charge, or a cracked case.

The primer must be seated flush against the head of the case. If the primer protrudes even a small amount, it can cause problems in revolvers. Depending on the location of the high-primer cartridge in the cylinder, it may prevent the cylinder from closing or may prevent the cylinder from rotating once it is closed. It will also be difficult to push the cylinder open while holding the cylinder release latch if a primer is pressing against the inside back of the frame.

If there is no powder in a case, or just a small amount of powder, the primer may cause enough force to push the bullet out of the case, but not enough force to push it all the way through and out the bore. This is called a squib. The bullet will be lodged part-way down the bore, creating a dangerous situation if the gun is fired again. The handgun will have to be unloaded and the bullet removed from the barrel.

Powder charges are carefully calculated to match the caliber, bullet weight, and type of powder. If a cartridge has a double powder charge, it can create a dangerous overload. The result could damage the handgun or cause injury to the shooter.

Sometimes a hand-loader loads a cracked case. If it is fired, the case may split open and expand. It will be difficult to remove from the chamber.

WHAT TO CARRY

To decide what is the best firearm to carry, you need to consider the following:

1. Your proficiency and training with firearms
2. The laws in your state
3. The potential dangers for and security needs of your principal
4. The number of people in your detail
5. Other special elements of the situation

You should assess all of these factors for each situation that you may encounter. You can always improve the first criterion by taking classes and by practice on the range. You should keep up to date with changes regarding the second criterion. The other three you will need to evaluate on an ongoing basis.

After you analyze these criteria, you will need to choose between a revolver and a semiautomatic. There are good and bad features of each. Which you choose will depend on your abilities and situation, and your decision may be for a revolver in one situation and a semiautomatic in another.

Revolvers generally have a smaller capacity than semiautomatics, holding only 5 or 6 rounds compared with up to 20. Revolvers are slower to reload than semiautomatics. Revolvers sometimes are bulkier and slightly more difficult to conceal than semiautomatics. Likewise, flat magazines are easier to conceal and carry than speed loaders. Revolvers are easier to learn to use and to use than semiautomatics and for rookie EPPs may be the better choice. Likewise, revolvers can be used by others in your party, even your principal, in an emergency. Many small revolvers with short barrels can be easily carried concealed, while equally small semiautomatics may be of too small a caliber or not as mechanically reliable because of their size. Revolvers can be easily made to comfortably fit your hand by changing the grip, while it is virtually impossible to make a semiautomatic fit your hand if it doesn't already. Revolvers tend to function without malfunction (as long as you keep them clean), while virtually all semiautomatics will malfunction at least once in their life. Revolvers are all alike in design, so anyone who knows how can use any revolver; semiautomatics are all different, and it is not easy for anyone but an expert to use a different semiautomatic without taking a bit of time to examine the differences.

Another consideration in your choice of handgun is the caliber. Generally, experts recommend that the minimum caliber for self-defense is .38 Special or 9 mm. What you choose will depend on whether you choose a revolver or semiautomatic, the laws in your state that may restrict what you carry, and the potential for danger in your assignment.

You may want to carry a second gun. Why? Your gun may malfunction or run out of ammunition. You may lose your gun in a struggle. You may not be able to reach your primary gun because you are holding something, are fighting, or are injured. You may want to pass a gun to another person in your party who isn't armed.

You will also need to carry extra ammunition. You should choose the same brand of ammunition as you carry in the handgun itself so you will know that the gun will continue to operate smoothly. You should carry extra ammunition in a speed loader or magazine and not loose in your pocket so you can reload as quickly as possible. Carry as much extra ammunition as you can conceal.

HOW TO CARRY A FIREARM

How you carry a firearm will depend on your body size and type, how you dress, and the type of firearm you carry. There is no one best way for everyone or every situation. The most important considerations are the following:

1. The firearm remains concealed at all times.
2. The firearm is safely contained so it won't accidentally fall out.
3. You have easy and quick access to draw the firearm.
4. It is comfortable to wear for long periods.

It may take some trial and error with equipment before you find what is best for you.

Start with the best equipment you can. A $15 nylon holster won't last as long as a $75 leather holster and won't secure your gun as well. If possible, find a good holster maker and have something custom made that fits your gun and your body. Remember, however, if you get a new gun, you will need a new holster.

There are six ways you can carry a gun: in a shoulder holster, in a belt holster, in an ankle holster, in a pocket, in a "fanny" pack, and in a briefcase. There are advantages and disadvantages to each.

Shoulder holsters may look good in the movies, but they tend to be uncomfortable for many people and not practical for women. It is difficult to conceal the leather strapping and connectors on your back and shoulders. You may need to have a special jacket made to cover the bulges under your arms (gun in the holster and ammunition pouches). The draw tends to be slow and requires that you swing the gun muzzle in a wide arc before getting it on target.

A belt holster can be worn in many places. The most comfortable position for most people is over their shooting-hand kidney with the gun butt toward the small of the back. The gun can be reached and drawn with either hand from this position. This is also the fastest concealed draw. Only those with a slim waist can wear the holster on the shooting-hand side or in front for a cross-draw, but both of these locations make it more difficult to keep the gun concealed.

Ankle holsters are often uncomfortable, and they "show" when your pant leg rides up as you step out of a car, sit, cross your legs, or go up stairs. The draw is slow since it requires pulling your pant leg up with your support hand as you kneel on your other knee, and drawing the gun from the inside of your opposite ankle with your shooting hand. You must then shoot from a kneeling position, which may not always be the most efficient way if people are moving.

Carrying a firearm in a pocket is generally not the best plan since it moves around, creates a lump that may show the gun, and causes your clothing to hang, showing you have something heavy in your pocket. The draw is slow from a pocket and generally causes you to point the muzzle at your body. You can shoot through a pocket with most small guns, but you won't have any accuracy.

"Fanny" packs are a popular and comfortable way to carry a firearm, but they are good only when you are wearing casual clothing. You can carry every size of handgun and extra ammunition in specially designed packs that have a tear-away front that conceals a holstered gun.

Carrying your firearm in a briefcase should only be done if you don't expect to be attacked, since it would be very slow to "draw" your gun. It also requires you to use one hand to carry the briefcase, which lessens your options for other forms of self-defense. It can be a good way, however, to transport firearms to a location such as a hotel or meeting room.

DEFENSIVE SHOOTING

You can't learn defensive shooting from a book. You will need to take lessons, practice at a range, practice fast reloads with your firearms, practice your draw, and imagine various scenarios. You can obtain some semirealistic practice by playing paint-ball games with your friends and colleagues. You can also get proficient with drawing and shooting if you compete in matches with the United States Practical Shooting Association, which sponsors local International Practical Shooting Confederation (IPSC) matches across the country. Phone 360-855-2245 for information about clubs in your area.

CLEANING YOUR HANDGUN

Frequency

If you keep your handgun clean, it will operate at its best and won't have any of the malfunctions associated with poor maintenance. A good rule to follow is to clean your handgun every time you use it. If you plan to clean it after every five hundred rounds, for example, you probably won't keep track of how many rounds you shoot and won't clean it according to your planned schedule. The result will be lack of cleaning and a lot of residue buildup in your handgun.

Cleaning Kit

Make your own cleaning kit. You will need to supplement any kit you buy by adding some additional items. Make it small enough to keep in a case that you will always take with you. Take your cleaning kit to the range so you can clean your gun there before you reload it and go back out onto the street or back to work. You will want to combine all the items you get into a basic cleaning kit, with special kits for each caliber of handgun you have. A basic cleaning kit should include (1) nylon bristle and stainless steel brushes; (2) a rod in segments; (3) patch holders that screw into the rod; (4) a dental pick; (5) nitro solvent; and (6) gun oil.

The special kit for each caliber should include bore brushes in the correct caliber. For a semiautomatic pistol you need two bore brushes, one brass and one stainless steel. For a revolver you need two sets, a long one to use on the chambers and a short one to use on the bore, one set in brass and one set in stainless steel. The kit should also include patches of a size that will fit through the bore. Keep the special kit for each caliber in a zip-lock plastic bag. You could put a card in each bag with the caliber written on it for easy reference.

Gun-cleaning Safety

Follow all the rules of safe gun handling while you are cleaning your gun. Before you start to clean your handgun, unload it and put all live ammunition in another room or away from the area you are using for cleaning. Recheck to make sure the gun is unloaded. Clean your handgun in a place where you are alone and won't be pointing the muzzle at someone else.

Cleaning a Revolver

Most of the problems with revolvers come from poor maintenance that allows lead shavings and gunpowder residue to build up around the forcing cone, under the star, in the chambers, and in the bore. Cleaning your revolver every time you shoot, no matter how many or few rounds you shoot, will eliminate these problems. The bore and cylinder will have residue and blow-back from the discharge. There will also be residue inside the bottom of the frame and the front of the cylinder. If you shoot lead bullets, there will also be lead shavings on the forcing cone and in the bore.

Start by cleaning the bore. (1) Look inside. If it is a mirrored surface, it won't need the heavy stainless brush, as double passes with the brass bore brush will suffice. Use the short brush so it will pass all the way through the bore into the cylinder opening. (2) Dip the bore brush into the solvent, then push it all the way through the bore. (3) Be careful that you don't strike the rod against the edge of the muzzle. This can cause scratches that will affect the accuracy of the gun. Also, be careful not to push the end of the bore brush against the firing pin on the inside back of the frame. Place a folded patch or small piece of leather over this area to help protect it. (4) Push the brush all the way through the bore so the bristles all leave the bore. If you do this, you won't be trying to pull the bore brush out with the bristles bent backwards inside the bore.

Wherever you put solvent, it has to come off. Don't let solvent run down inside the revolver; it won't come out by itself. Hold the revolver so solvent doesn't run down inside the hole around the firing pin.

Clean around the forcing cone. Dip a brush into solvent and brush this area. Then clean it, using a dental pick to remove small lead shavings. Then brush it again. Next, use the patch holder on the rod and the proper size patch. Run it through the bore a few times. It will come out dirty. Keep changing the patch until one comes out clean. Then use clean patches around the forcing cone and wipe this area until the patches come off clean. Use the long bore brush in the chambers. There are two reasons for this. First, after cleaning the bore, the brush you used will be compressed and won't clean as well. Second, the chambers are much dirtier than the bore since this is where the cartridge detonates. The brush will get very dirty, and you shouldn't use it on the bore the next time you clean the revolver. If you use a long bore brush in the chambers, you will easily tell it apart from the short bore brush.

It doesn't matter which direction you clean the chambers from, front or back. Dip the brush into the solvent and run the brush all the way through and back a couple of times in each chamber. Clean any residue from under the star. Use a dental pick around each space under the star and follow this with the nylon brush. Then run clean, dry patches through each chamber, changing them until they come out clean from each one. Wipe off the whole cylinder including the ejector rod and the area under the star with clean patches.

Clean off the frame with solvent on a bristle brush. Wipe it clean with patches. Brush around the trigger with a nylon brush.

Put a few drops of oil on a patch and push it through the bore, then wipe it on the frame and cylinder. Don't leave excess oil on the gun because it will attract dust and lint. Take it off with a clean patch. Put a drop of oil on the shaft under the star and one drop on the front of the extractor rod. Work the rod a few times, then wipe off any excess oil. Wipe off all the cleaning equipment and put it away.

Cleaning a Semiautomatic Pistol

You need to disassemble a semiautomatic pistol to clean it. Follow the instructions in your manual. You only need to remove the slide, barrel, guide rod, and guide-rod spring. Clean the barrel first. Look inside the bore. If it is a mirrored surface, it won't need the heavy stainless brush; double passes with the brass bore brush will suffice. Dip the bore brush into the solvent, then push it all the way through the bore. Push the brush all the way through the bore so the bristles all leave the bore. If you do this, you won't be trying to pull the bore brush out with the bristles bent backwards.

Next, use the patch holder on the rod and the proper size patch. Run it through the bore a few times. It will come out dirty. Keep changing the patch until one comes out clean. Wipe off the outside of the barrel with a clean patch.

Next, clean the slide using a bristle brush dipped into solvent. Clean all along the guide rails. Use a dental pick on the area around the firing pin; there will be a lot of residue buildup. Use a bristle brush in this area. Finally, clean off the solvent with clean patches.

Wipe the guide rod and guide-rod spring with patches, wiping off any residue and oil. Wipe clean any other parts that you need to disassemble for your pistol. Using a brush dipped into solvent, clean the frame, the area around the hammer, the areas along the rails, and other exposed parts. Be careful that solvent doesn't run into parts where it will be difficult to remove it. Use the dental pick to remove residue buildup. Remove the solvent with patches until the patches lift off clean. Brush around the trigger with a nylon brush. Wipe inside the magazine well with patches.

Put a few drops of oil on a patch and push it through the bore, then wipe it on the barrel, guide rod, slide, and frame. Don't leave excess oil on the gun because it will attract dust and lint. Take it off with a clean patch. Reassemble the barrel into the slide. Put a drop of oil on each rail, then reassemble the slide onto the frame. Rack the slide back and forth a few times to disperse the oil. Wipe off all excess oil. Wipe off all the cleaning equipment and put it away.

SUGGESTED READING

This section lists a few of the many good books on the subject of firearms and shooting.

Shooting

The following books are published by Police Bookshelf, Concord, N.H. (800-624-9049).

In the Gravest Extreme, by Massad Ayoob

Stressfire, by Massad Ayoob

Stressfire II, by Massad Ayoob

Law

All of the following books are published by Bloomfield Press, Phoenix, AZ (800-707-4020) and contain gun laws that everyone needs to know.

Gun Laws of America, by Alan Korwin (all the federal gun laws)
The Arizona Gun Owner's Guide, by Alan Korwin
The California Gun Owner's Guide, by Georgene Lockwood and Alan Korwin
The Florida Gun Owner's Guide, by Donna Lea Hawley and Alan Korwin
The Texas Gun Owner's Guide, by Alan Korwin and Georgene Lockwood
The Virginia Gun Owner's Guide, by Alan Korwin and Steve Maniscalco

14

First Aid

First aid is an important skill for everyone in the executive protection profession. If you don't already have first-aid certification, it is imperative that you take a course and become certified. Make sure the course you take has both first aid for injuries and illness and a cardiopulmonary resuscitation (CPR) component like those offered at the American Red Cross. Once you are certified, renew your certification each year so you are always current with the latest techniques.

You should know how to handle virtually every type of first-aid emergency that may occur to help your principal, others who are in your party, and yourself. For example, your principal could have a heart attack during a business meeting, get something in his eye on a windy day, or have an allergic reaction after being stung by a bee. An agent may suffer from heat exhaustion while keeping watch outside on a hot summer day or be cut by an attacker with a knife. You may be cut, shot, or injured in a fight. Learning first aid will give you the added confidence that comes from knowing what to do in a medical emergency. This will help you keep calm and maintain control in that situation. Knowing how to analyze a medical emergency and take the proper steps will help you to keep the victim alive and prevent injuries from becoming a worse threat.

Of course, you will only attend to first aid after an emergency situation is over and there is no further possibility of danger. Likewise, you should never leave your principal unattended while you perform first aid on a bystander or other person not under your protection. This may be harsh, but your entire responsibility is to your principal.

You need to have a plan for first aid in the same way you have a plan for all other aspects of your job as an EPP. Your first-aid plan will have three parts: planning, prevention, and response. This chapter will discuss how to create a first-aid plan and present some basic first-aid responses to situations that you may encounter. This book is not a substitute for taking a course, but a guide to the types of actions you may take in a first-aid situation.

YOUR FIRST-AID PLAN

Planning is the first step and includes anticipating the types of first-aid emergencies that may arise, preparation of a first-aid kit, and training those who will respond. When you search vehicles and locations, include a safety survey for anything that may cause an injury or facilitate an unhealthy situation and ask yourself questions such as whether there are uneven surfaces that may cause your principal to trip. Survey your principal and other members of your party and find out if anyone has any medical problems such as diabetes or a heart condition. Is anyone on regular or periodic medication? Think of all the possible types of attacks that are possible in the facilities or vehicles you will be using. Could you be subject to a bomb, a crushing crowd, a gunshot, or a fan with scissors who wants a lock of hair?

Write out a list of the types of first-aid emergencies that could possibly occur for each situation that you may encounter. Pack a first-aid kit for each situation and keep one in each vehicle and a small one on your person. Review your kit for each new situation and keep it stocked with fresh materials. Keep a supply of latex gloves in your kit and on your person to protect yourself from blood-transmitted diseases. Let everyone with security clearance know where the first-aid kit is and keep it in an accessible location so it can be recovered quickly.

On your route map and in your site planning include all emergency medical facilities, the types of services they offer, their hours, and the best route to them. Make sure your drivers know these.

Make medical information cards or sheets for your principal, the principal's family members, yourself, and all members of your detail. List information such as name, age, allergies, brief medical history, medications used, wearing of contact lenses or glasses, insurance information, doctor's name and phone number, dentist's name and phone number, and next-of-kin information. Keep one of these on your person, one in the main bag or suitcase for the detail, and one with a second person. Each person should carry a copy of his or her own medical information card.

Plan for hospital visits. If you are a single EPP with one principal, plan to accompany your injured principal to the hospital and to remain with or near the principal during examination and treatment. If you have a detail, appoint one or two people to this task. Likewise, plan what you will do if you are injured. Who will look after your principal? If you are a sole EPP, keep an emergency card in your wallet that gives phone numbers of whom to call if you are unconscious. If you work with a detail, plan who will take over your duties if you are injured. Also, plan for the security of firearms and other emergency equipment carried by an injured person who may need to go to a hospital. It will usually be best to safely remove these items before medical help arrives.

When dealing with paramedics, doctors, and other medical professionals, explain why you are with the injured principal and your need to maintain security. Ask where you may stay so you don't get in their way but can still do your job. Clearly explain any continuing danger or threat that may cause further injury to your principal or the medical people. Provide them with all the medical information they need about the injured person, but don't give out any information that may compromise the security or safety of your principal.

Prevention is the second step in your first-aid plan. Prevention is always better than trying to deal with a first-aid emergency. First-aid prevention should become part of your overall plan as an EPP to prevent harm coming to your principal. You already plan to prevent your principal from being injured by an attacker; you should also plan to prevent medical emergencies from happening. Tripping and spraining an ankle, getting cut on a broken glass in a bathroom, or having a heart attack can result in as much harm to your principal's life, activities, and peace of mind as a physical attack.

Response is the third step. No matter how much you anticipate and try to prevent them, accidents and injuries can occur. If you have a first-aid kit available and trained people ready to use it, you will be able to respond quickly and appropriately. First aid is immediate, temporary care of an injured person until medical attention is available. First aid involves basic procedures only. You are not a doctor and shouldn't take action that you are unqualified to perform unless it is to save the life of someone who will die without your immediate action. You should always follow the standard procedures that you learn in your first aid. Always get professional medical attention for the injured person, even if that person feels at the time that he or she doesn't want it or if the injury appears to be minor because you may not have recognized a more serious injury. The following sections present some basic first-aid procedures for injuries that may occur in an EPP situation and some examples of standard procedures.

CUTS AND SCRAPES

Scrapes remove the outer layer of skin and leave an area where dirt and other materials can enter and cause infection. Clean scrapes with soap and water, then bandage to avoid further problems.

Cuts caused by sharp objects or from hits with a blunt object usually bleed freely. They may not be painful if nerve damage has occurred. To control bleeding, cover the wound with a dressing and apply direct pressure. If the cut continues to bleed, elevate the injured limb above the victim's heart. If the wound continues to bleed, add more dressings on top of those already on the wound and call for medical assistance. While you wait for help to arrive, reduce the flow of blood to the injured area by squeezing an artery against a bone at a pressure point. Pressure points are located under the biceps on the upper arm and where the leg bends at the hip. Whenever you are giving first aid and blood is present, remember to wear latex gloves from the first-aid kit to protect yourself from any blood-borne diseases.

HEAD INJURIES

When someone sustains a head injury, you cannot tell if he or she has suffered brain damage or if there is internal bleeding that is putting pressure on nerve endings. Therefore, treat all head injuries seriously. Whenever someone loses consciousness, call 911. Time how long the victim is unconscious. The duration of unconsciousness is important information needed by the paramedics. Always make sure someone stays with an unconscious person and monitors him or her until medical help arrives. Don't try to move an unconscious person because he or she may have a neck injury. It is important, however, that you make sure that the victim has a clear airway and can breathe. If he or she regains consciousness, don't let him or her get up. While he or she is lying down, talk to him or her. Try to get him or her to relax because people often get excitable as their brain function starts to come back. While you are waiting for the paramedics, monitor his or her answers so you can update them on his or her condition.

You should know some general information about different types of concussions that may occur. If someone is stunned or dazed by a hit to the head and doesn't lose consciousness, he or she may experience short-term memory loss, headache, and temporary blurred vision. With the exception of the headache, these will all come back to normal quite quickly. At the least, have the person rest before continuing any activity.

If someone loses consciousness for 1 to 10 seconds, he or she has suffered a first-degree concussion. When he or she regains consciousness, he or she can expect a headache, short-term memory loss, blurred vision, and dizziness or unsteadiness. When someone suffers this type of injury, ask him or her, "Do you know what happened?" "What day is it?" and "Do you know where you are?" If the person answers correctly, he or she is starting to recover, but don't let him or her get right up. Have him or her sit up slowly. After a few minutes, help him or her stand up. A second-degree concussion occurs when a person loses consciousness between a time length of ten seconds and four minutes. Any unconsciousness more than four minutes indicates a third-degree concussion. Stay with the person until medical assistance arrives.

EYE INJURIES

Eye injuries can be minor, such as a bruised eyeball, or quite severe, such as a detached retina, but you should treat all eye injuries as severe because of the potential loss of eyesight. The following are some general guidelines:

Never let anyone rub an injured eye. If a person suffers an eye injury, perspiration or tears may get into the eyes and cause a considerable amount of stinging. Don't confuse this with other problems. Use a towel to gently wipe the perspiration away from the eyes. When a person gets hit in the eye, he or she may experience blurred vision or a loss of vision. These conditions should be temporary, depending on the force and angle of the blow.

If the victim suffers a scratched cornea, get him or her to an eye doctor immediately. A scratched cornea feels like you have something in your eye when it is closed. If this happens, cover the injured eye with gauze or a patch to help keep it closed and take the victim to a doctor.

If the victim suffers from a cheekbone fracture, a "blowout" fracture occurs. The victim won't be able to control his or her eye. Cover both eyes to prevent the good eye from moving, because if the good eye moves, the injured eye will try to move along with it, which can be painful. Get the victim to a hospital immediately.

If a person is hit hard enough straight on, he or she may suffer a detached retina. It is difficult, if not impossible, for anyone except an expert to tell if this has happened. If, after such a blow, the victim has double vision, blurred vision, a loss of vision, or difficulty focusing on close objects, get him or her to the hospital immediately.

NOSEBLEEDS

Nosebleeds may occur after a person is hit on the nose or for other reasons. You can control the bleeding by placing an ice pack on the bridge of the nose. Always have the person tilt his or her head forward and never back. This will cause any blood to flow out of the nostrils instead of back down the person's throat, which may make him or her sick.

DISLOCATIONS AND FRACTURES

Without an X ray you can't know if an injury is a dislocation or a fracture, so it is usually best to assume that it is a fracture. Keep the injured person warm, reassure him or her that help is on the way, and don't do anything to the injury. If you think that someone has suffered from a fracture or dislocation, call 911 and take the following steps while you wait for medical help to arrive:

If the injury is to a finger or toe, don't try to adjust the joint into place. Instead, put an ice pack on the injury. This will help reduce the swelling, help lessen pain, decrease bleeding at the injury site, and generally stop the injury from getting worse. Encourage the victim to hold the injured limb in a comfortable position and have someone stay with the victim to reassure him or her and help keep him or her calm.

If the injury is to an elbow or knee, it is a major emergency because the blood flow to the injured area is probably going to be cut off. Don't move a victim who has an elbow or knee injury because you can cause nerve damage, rip blood vessels, or cause more bleeding. You can put an ice pack over the injury, but this won't be as helpful as it is for a smaller injury. Keep the victim warm and talk to him or her calmly until medical help arrives. Don't raise the victim's head or legs if he or she has an elbow or knee injury, but let him or her sit or lie in a comfortable position.

GUNSHOT WOUNDS

Three characteristics of gunshot wounds make them particularly serious. They are all dirty injuries. Because they are blast injuries, the extent of damage cannot be known until they are explored at a hospital. If there is injury to a blood vessel, the wound may bleed heavily. For any gunshot wound, call 911 for immediate medical help. While you wait for medical help to arrive, control the bleeding and prevent any further damage to the injury. Don't forget to wear latex gloves when handling any bleeding injury.

Use gauze pads directly over the wound and apply direct pressure to control bleeding. Add more gauze pads or other clean absorbent material on top of the existing ones if the bleeding continues. If the injury is in a limb, immobilize the limb and have the victim lie down and remain still. Don't move the victim unless you have to get him or her away from a dangerous situation to avoid further injury. Use an ice pack to help reduce swelling around the injured area. Keep the victim calm, prevent him or her from moving around, and treat him or her for shock if necessary while you wait for medical help to arrive. If the victim has been shot in the chest and you can hear air rushing in and out of the wound as the victim breathes, use a plastic sheet or pad to cover the wound and use pressure to hold it over the wound to prevent the air movement.

CONCLUSION

Remember that first aid is only immediate and temporary assistance while you wait for medical help to arrive. For most injury situations, this is the best course of action. However, in an EPP situation that involves an attack in a public place, an unruly crowd that continues to present a danger, an explosion in a vehicle or building, or some other danger that continues to threaten further injury or death to your principal, your only course of action may be to remove an injured person, either to another site to provide first aid or to a hospital, providing first aid during transportation to the hospital. The situation, type and severity of the injury, life-threatening nature of the injury, and size of your detail will all factor into your decision of how to provide first aid.

You must take the best first-aid courses you can find and keep your first-aid certification current. Even with this, recognize that first-aid training is minimal training and prepares you only to perform basic help until medical help is available. Always get qualified medical help as soon as possible for every first-aid and medical emergency. Apparently small injuries can become life-threatening dangers without proper treatment.

15

Equipment

An EPP needs to carry the right equipment to do the job, but not so much as to have excess baggage. Certain equipment will always be needed. Other equipment will vary depending on the principal, places you are going, level of threat expected, and mode of transportation used. For example, if your principal has a medical condition, the equipment may include a backup prescription or list of local emergency centers; if you are going to be outdoors in bad weather, you may need extra rain gear; if the level of threat is very low or you are going on a commercial airplane, you may choose not to wear a firearm. Every situation will be different, and deciding on the equipment that you will need will be part of your evaluation and preparation for the job.

EMERGENCY EQUIPMENT

Emergency equipment that you may need can be divided into six different categories: standard equipment, vehicle emergencies, first-aid and medical emergencies, self-defense, documents, and accidents. Some items of emergency equipment will be useful in more than one category.

Choose your clothing so it has pockets or a belt that will easily and comfortably hold and conceal all the emergency equipment that you may need. You should be able to carry emergency equipment in such a way that it doesn't move around when you walk or sit, doesn't fall out if you run or bend over, and is easy to remove and use. Use bags or cases for emergency equipment only when they can be left in a vehicle or when you can carry a bag without reducing your ability to respond to an emergency and, if possible, in a manner that will allow you to keep your hands free.

STANDARD EQUIPMENT

Standard equipment that you will require and should always have with you will include items such as the following:

- Driver license and other personal identification
- EPP license (where and when it is required by law)
- Firearms and concealed-carry license

- Letter or other appointment from your principal
- Money and credit cards
- List of emergency contacts
- Small flashlight
- Umbrella
- Extra keys to motor vehicle and buildings
- Pager or cell phone

You may need documentation of these types for a variety of reasons from checking into a hotel to showing a law-enforcement officer that you may carry the weapon you have in your possession. Extra keys will eliminate delays caused by a misplaced key. A small flashlight will help you at night or in a dark location. A cell phone will keep you in touch with your contacts and will be useful in an emergency.

You also need to carry your own personal items. If you wear glasses or contact lenses, always carry a second pair. If you are allergic to anything, wear a medic alert tag or carry a small amount of medication for an emergency. If you are a sole agent and not part of a team or detail, you may need to carry extra items such as a small first-aid kit.

VEHICLE EMERGENCIES

The best response for vehicle emergencies is prevention. Make sure that all vehicles are in good working order. This includes checking to see that the engine is in good repair, vehicles have good tires that are properly inflated, fuel tanks are full, all other fluid levels are full, door locks and windows are working properly, windows and mirrors are clean for good vision, seat belts are in good working order, the car phone is working, and so on.

If the vehicle breaks down for any reason from a flat tire to an improperly working door lock, don't try to repair it yourself, especially if you are the sole agent. Call for a replacement vehicle that you have inspected and have on standby for emergencies, and stay with your principal in a safe place or locked vehicle until the replacement vehicle arrives. If you are in a motorcade, transfer the people in the disabled vehicle into one of the other vehicles so you don't lose time or have to remain stationary for long. Leave someone with the disabled vehicle until a replacement vehicle arrives, but let the rest of the detail continue with the motorcade.

If the vehicle has a flat tire, you can drive on it for a considerable distance to get to help if you have no backup vehicle available. This will probably destroy the rim, but at least you will keep moving instead of being a stationary target. If the engine fails, you will have to wait for help. Make sure your cell phone is not dependent on the vehicle's battery and that door locks will work without power from the vehicle's battery or engine.

Only as a last resort should you try to repair the vehicle yourself. You should only do this if (1) there is no backup vehicle available, (2) you are not in a motorcade, and (3) you need to get to your destination without delay. Keep the principal secured in the vehicle while you change the tire or make any repair that you are able to do to get the vehicle moving again. Be wary of any stranger who offers assistance because he or she may be someone who has sabotaged your vehicle and wants to get to your principal to harm or annoy him or her. You should call for law-enforcement assistance whenever you are stranded and need to make repairs or wait for backup to alert them of your situation and location.

FIRST-AID AND MEDICAL EMERGENCIES

First aid is covered in chapter 14, but we will discuss here what types of equipment you may want to include in your vehicle and on your person for first-aid and medical emergencies. You should keep a good first-aid kit in a well-marked, secure container in the vehicle. It should include items such as the following:

- Sterile gauze bandages in various sizes
- Roller bandages
- Tweezers
- Cold packs
- Latex gloves
- Antibacterial soap
- Container of distilled water (for washing small wounds)
- Blanket
- Plastic or vinyl bandages/patches for sucking chest wounds
- Medication prescribed for principal or any member of detail

In addition to a large first-aid kit, you should keep a few gauze pads in their sterile wrappers with the personal equipment you carry for immediate response to a wound.

SELF-DEFENSE EQUIPMENT

Self-defense equipment usually will consist of firearms or nonlethal weapons. You should take only those items that may be necessary to meet the most severe risk you expect and that are legal for the place you will be.

Firearms

Carrying a firearm as emergency equipment will depend on the type of principal, level of risk expected, and destinations. If you carry a firearm, you will also need extra ammunition and a good holster and belt. We have discussed the types of firearms and how to carry them in chapter 13.

You will need to carry extra ammunition. With revolvers, the decision to carry extra ammunition is usually easy to make because of the limited capacity of five or six rounds, but even if you have a high-capacity auto-loader, carrying extra ammunition is usually a good choice. What if you carry a semiautomatic and in a struggle for the gun the magazine release is pushed and you lose the magazine? What if this is the moment that your magazine spring decides to fail, or your gun decides that it doesn't like to feed the ammunition you have in it? What if the encounter turns out to be more than you ever expected and you run out of ammunition? An extra magazine of ammunition can save the day (and your principal's life).

You may want a second gun. It is often difficult to properly conceal one gun without thinking about where to carry a second one, but carrying a second gun can be a good decision. If your gun breaks or malfunctions in a way that you can't easily and quickly fix, you can use the second gun. A second gun can also be the fastest way to reload, especially if you carry a revolver and haven't practiced speed-loading it. It can also be a great way to carry extra ammunition. If you lose your gun in a struggle, or the attacker has taken it from you somehow, you still have your second gun that can make the difference between the life and death of your principal and yourself. There may be a time when you are in a position where you can't reach your gun to draw it. It is stuck under your jacket and strapped under the car's seat belt. The attacker has surprised you and has grabbed your shooting hand and you can't draw. Your shooting hand or arm has been injured in the first assault and you can't draw. If you carry your second gun on a different part of your body and where you can reach it with either hand, you still have a way to get at a weapon.

Nonlethal Weapons

Carrying nonlethal weapons will depend on your ability and expertise in their use and the local laws. Some martial arts–style weapons are illegal in some states, so you should check the laws of the areas you will travel in to see if you can take the weapons you prefer. It may also be illegal to conceal nonlethal weapons in some states. Your concealed-firearms license may not include other forms of weapons. Again, check the local laws. You cannot protect your principal if you are in the police station explaining why you are carrying nunchaku.

DOCUMENTS

Documents are a part of our life, and it is important that you have ready access to any type of document that you or your principal will need. You need to carry as standard equipment documents such as your driver license and other personal identification, your EPP license, your firearms and concealed-carry license, a letter or other appointment from your principal, money and credit cards, medical insurance card, a list of emergency contacts, your passport for international travel, and a photocopy of each of these in a waterproof wrapper in a different location on your person. In addition to these, you will need to carry certain documents for your principal and for travel. These will include items such as the following:

- Confirmation of hotel reservations
- Airline tickets and boarding cards
- A schedule of travel and meetings, including addresses, contact people, and phone numbers
- A photocopy of each of your principal's personal documents in a waterproof wrapper
- Copies of vehicle registration and insurance documents

You should keep all documents in order so that you may produce them when needed without using more than one hand and without taking too much of your attention away from your main job of providing security for your principal. If you are in a detail, assign this task to another member.

ACCIDENTS

All sorts of complications can occur from a major automobile accident involving injury and requiring complex extraction from vehicles to your principal spilling coffee on his or her clothing. For major accidents, probably the best emergency equipment you can carry will be your cell phone. You can call for help and undertake whatever first aid you can until help arrives.

For small accidents, you can have gauze pads for scrapes and cuts. A sharp pocket knife that you can easily open with one hand is useful to cut things such as seat belts, wrappings, or snagged clothing. If you always carry a pocket knife, remember to remove it and put it with checked baggage before you fly on a commercial airline. You don't want to get delayed at a security checkpoint over a 3-inch blade while your principal is crowded on into the terminal area without you. In restaurants and public places notice where towels and other items that may be useful in a mishap are located so you can ask someone to get them for you to hand to your principal.

If the problem involves something like a forgotten briefcase, your listing of meeting places and phone numbers will allow you to phone to get someone to retrieve the forgotten or misplaced item and bring it to you. If you are traveling by automobile, you may want to keep a fresh set of clothing, including shoes and socks, in case you get caught in the rain or step into a puddle. You can quickly change while another detail member watches the principal so you are presentable to accompany him or her anywhere. An umbrella will provide cover for your principal in the rain, but when you are working with a detail, don't hold it yourself if you are the personal security officer. You need your hands free for emergencies.

16

Develop a Training Program

As an EPP, it is important that you develop your defensive tactics and handgun skills to the highest level possible. You can't do this without practice, and you can't get the best practice unless you develop a training program for yourself. This chapter presents some elements that you should include in your training program for defensive tactics and disarming techniques. Practice sessions for shooting are covered in the chapter on firearms.

SAFETY

If you are practicing defensive tactics or disarming techniques, safety is an important element to include in your practice sessions. You don't want to get injured while training. You won't be able to protect your principal if you are in the hospital or have a broken arm. You also don't want to hurt anyone else during training.

Never practice disarming techniques with real firearms. If you practice with a real handgun, you will develop the bad habit of pointing the muzzle at other people, at yourself, and in unsafe directions. You will get used to "playing" with your handgun and may slip and do this at other times when you aren't in a practice session and when the gun is loaded.

Before you start a practice session on disarming techniques, take all firearms and ammunition out of the room. Unload the firearms even though they won't be used in the practice session. You will be practicing handling firearms in an "unsafe" manner, so you don't want loaded ones within reach after your practice session begins. After your session, loading the real firearms will help you refocus your mind that practice is over and now you are really armed again.

Use practice guns for disarming techniques. It is best to use cast aluminum or something similar to give the feel of the weight and size of your handgun. You can also use plastic waterguns, toy guns, and plywood cutouts that you make yourself. Sand rough edges off practice guns to protect your hands and clothing. You can also reinforce practice guns with tape.

Remove all types of weapons from your body before you start. Remove knives, jodons, pens, spare magazines, and any similar items from your pockets, belt, and ankle holster. You and your practice partner should do a pat-down on each other to find anything you don't notice because you are so used to wearing it. You need to do this to prevent you from automatically reaching for a weapon if you get into an intense struggle during the practice session. It will also prevent injuries from falling or banging on a hard object in your pocket.

Use inexpensive holsters, not your expensive carry holster. Try one of a similar design to the one you normally wear. Use an inexpensive nylon pancake holster to replace your more expensive leather one, for example. You will be more willing to severely pull and struggle with a practice holster because it won't matter if it is damaged. Likewise, the practice gun won't stretch your carry holster.

Never put your finger into the trigger guard of a practice gun; it could get injured when the gun is ripped from your hand during training. You could wear gloves during practice, but this won't give you the feel of a real-life situation where you probably won't be wearing gloves.

Use rubber knives, not hard plastic ones. A hard plastic knife can cut or cause abrasions. Get practice knives of different sizes and styles so you get used to facing a variety of cutting weapons. Also try to get one about the same size as you normally carry.

Make sure you have enough room to practice safely. If you are using an office, move the furniture so you have space to move around. Remove objects that may be broken if they are hit by a practice gun that is flung from your hands. If you are training on a tile floor, make sure you wear shoes that won't slip. If you aren't in a gym or martial arts facility, before you start to practice, close the blinds. You don't want neighbors or passersby calling the SWAT team to come and save you from your attacker.

SKILL DEVELOPMENT

To develop any physical techniques from tying your shoes or playing the piano to handgun retention, you need to develop the proper skills. This usually involves two stages, training and practice. Training is the instruction phase, which may include reading this book, watching a video, or taking a class. Training is usually a short phase that gives you the information on how to perform the skills. Practice is the stage that involves repeated performance of the movements to acquire skill proficiency.

You need to practice to be able to perform defensive tactics, defensive driving, handgun retention and disarming techniques, and any other physical skill you need to be an EPP. The way you practice, the number of repetitions of each skill, the number of practice sessions you have, and the overall length of time you practice all contribute to the competence you will develop.

The training stage of learning skills (reading a book, looking at pictures, watching a video, seeing a demonstration, performing a few repetitions in a class) will give you a brief exposure to the techniques, but none of these alone, or even in combination, is enough for you to learn physical skills well enough to perform them later. Brief exposures only put the skills into your short-term memory. Short-term memory stores information for a short time in your conscious mind. You can only do a physical skill by saying to yourself all the steps as you perform the technique. For example, you must say to yourself: he is holding a gun to my back with his right hand: first I do X, then I do Y, and then I do Z. This is what you need to do as you start to learn a physical skill.

If you just read a book or go to a class, you may be able to "walk through" the skills during the class, but you won't be able to remember how to do the skills later. You won't be able to perform the skills if someone holds you at gunpoint, throws a punch at you, or attacks you in any of the ways you learned. In an emergency, when your life and the life of your principal are on the line, you won't have time to try to remember each step in a technique and say each step to yourself in your conscious mind as you try to perform them.

To learn physical skills in such a way that you can perform them later without going through this step-by-step self-talk, you need to store the skills in your long-term memory. This means that they must be stored in your subconscious mind. Some people refer to this as creating muscle memory. You aren't really getting your muscles to remember anything. What you are doing is storing a sequence of nerve impulses in your brain and your central and peripheral nervous systems. When the skill memory is triggered, the nerves fire in the proper sequence to cause your muscles to contract to perform the desired skill. There are a number of basic practice techniques that you can use to develop your own sessions that will accomplish this result. The most important thing about practice, however, is repetition. Develop your own EPP skills practice sessions using the following practice methods:

1. Get a Practice Partner

Get a friend or associate who wants to develop the same skills as you as a practice partner. It doesn't matter if you are the same size or sex; it only matters that you both have the same attitude and commitment toward developing your skills. Practice partners must understand that their job is to help their partner learn and develop skills. Avoid anyone who thinks that he or she knows more than others, who wants to try to overpower or trick others to show that he or she is better, or who won't do new skills in a step-by-step manner but only wants to do them fast. Spouses and lovers generally make bad practice partners.

2. Schedule Sessions

Treat learning EPP defensive skills as a long-term matter and set regular practice sessions. Twice a week for a year is a good starting point. This seems like a lot of time, but it won't seem a waste of time if it saves your life or that of your principal. In order to perform a physical skill such as a disarming technique, a side kick, or any other skill, you will need to perform it perfectly a minimum of 3,000 times.

Pick a time that you can keep on a regular basis so that you won't have to constantly reschedule. If the time is inconvenient, you will probably stop practicing altogether. You only need to schedule an hour or two a week, but you must use all that time for practice, not for "getting ready" or gossip. Start and end on time.

3. Plan Each Session

Don't try to do everything in each session. Likewise, don't spend your session discussing what you want to do. Make a written list of things to do for at least the next five sessions. You can plan to do two skills the first session. In each subsequent session you can review the skills you have already learned and learn one new skill. After you have learned a number of skills, you can vary each session by focusing on two or three each time and adding a new skill every other or every third session. Vary your sessions by doing step-by-step practice, practicing skills with speed, using opponent resistance, adding surprise attacks, just performing multiple repetitions, and devoting some sessions to difficulties you are having.

4. Learning a New Skill or Technique

When you are learning a new skill or technique, the best way is to get a personal trainer. If one isn't available, use other materials. Carefully look at the book, video, notes, or material you have that describes the skill. Break the skill into its parts using this information. Do each step slowly in sequence a number of times by yourself without a partner. Then go through each step slowly with your partner. The "active" partner will be the person learning and doing the skill, and the "passive" partner will be the attacker. When you first start learning a new skill, have the passive partner read the steps out loud to the active partner as he or she does each step. Do each step exactly right. If you make a mistake, start again. Do the whole skill very slowly ten times, then let the other partner be the active partner and do it ten times.

Take turns doing the skill ten times. Complete each step more smoothly by flowing between the steps, but don't hurry, or you will get sloppy. You are going to do this thousands of times over the next year, so you don't need to do it fast at this stage. The passive partner should watch the active partner and see what he or she may be doing wrong. Watch for bending at the waist, feet in the wrong position, not stepping correctly, and so on. If you see something wrong, stop your partner and point it out. When your partner says "stop," don't move so he or she can show you how your body, leg, or arm is out of place.

5. Make It Smooth

When you get to the point where you can remember to do each step without thinking about the steps, start to make the steps flow together. You can speed up a bit, but don't rush it. Physical skills such as defensive techniques will often work better when they are done properly at a slower speed than when they are done quickly and sloppily. In an emergency, if they are properly embedded into your subconscious mind, you will automatically do them quickly. If you practice them fast too soon, you may become a bit sloppy on the technique, and you will be imprinting a sloppy technique in your brain. You will only be able to do it sloppily.

6.   Add Resistance and Surprise

Once you can do the defensive skills smoothly and quickly, you can have your partner add resistance and surprise. Make sure you discuss this with your partner at the start of your practice session. If your partner suddenly decides to resist you without telling you, one of you could get injured. Also, resistance without prior agreement can result in one person getting angry and striking back after the struggle is over. Surprise can be added to sessions by approaching from different angles, using crossover grabs, varying attack and nonattack approaches, randomly selecting attacks, and adding verbal insults or pleas.

7.   Vary Practice Partners

You will benefit most if you have a variety of practice partners. If you only practice with one person, you will soon learn each other's strengths, weaknesses, skills, strategies, energy levels, and other things that will cause you to respond the same way each session. This isn't ideal because your attacker won't be like your practice partner. If you use a variety of partners, you will get a greater benefit because you will have to respond to "attackers" who are larger, smaller, stronger, weaker, faster, or slower, and who combine these attributes with different strategies and energy in practice.

8.   Practice Both Right and Left Sides

You can't know if your real-life attacker will be right or left handed. It is critical that you be able to do each defensive skill and technique equally well against a right-handed or a left-handed attacker. If you learn from the right side, doing the technique from the left is just the mirror opposite, but it feels very different. After you have learned each technique reasonably well, learn it from the opposite side by taking the same slow step-by-step approach. At every practice session do an equal number of repetitions of each technique from both the right and left sides.

9.   Practice, Practice, Practice

Practice as often as you can. You can't learn defensive skills and techniques too well. Your life and the life of your principal depend on it.

17

Protection against Weapons

It is likely that at some time or other an EPP will encounter an armed attacker. It may be someone with scissors who wants a lock of your principal's hair or someone who has a gun and wants to kill your principal. Any situation where someone has any type of weapon is potentially very dangerous to your principal, yourself, and anyone else in the area. It is important that you learn and practice defensive techniques to deal with an armed attacker. It is also likely that you will encounter someone who wants to disarm you. Maintaining control of your own weapons is an equally important skill to learn. This chapter will outline some techniques for disarming an attacker and protecting your own weapon(s). You cannot learn these complex techniques by just reading a book. Take courses from a reputable instructor who has experience in this specific area of self-defense. Practice the techniques you learn until you can do them without thinking about each movement.

DISARMING AN ATTACKER

You may suddenly find that someone near you or your principal has a gun. This is an extremely dangerous situation, and you will have to act very quickly. It is possible to disarm someone with a gun, but you should only attempt this if you think that it is an immediate life-or-death situation. This chapter outlines some disarming techniques that you can practice. The principle of these techniques can also be used against an attacker with a knife.

Guns have the power to kill in a microsecond and from a distance. Upon recognition that a weapon has entered the equation, alert your fellow detail members and/or your principal by yelling the threat and direction of the intruder. Guns are far more dangerous than any unarmed attacker and can be used by, and generally are used by, people who are untrained. Guns can also kill by accident. Because of the ease with which a gun can kill you or an innocent bystander, using any self-defense or disarming technique is very dangerous. Take courses in these techniques and practice them often.

Any unarmed defense against an attacker with a gun should only be done if you are in a life-and-death situation where you feel and believe that the criminal is going to kill you right now. Forget all the Hollywood movie theatrics; they just don't work in the real world. In the real world the gun will kill or severely injure you in a flash. If you are farther away than arm's reach, forget trying any technique to take a gun away from an attacker. He can shoot you before you get to him; bullets travel much faster than you do. However, depending on the situation, how close you are, how jumpy he is, and if you really feel he is going to shoot you, you may be able to do something to get closer to him. Keeping your hands up and crying, "Please don't shoot me, I have two small children," while you shuffle toward him might get you close enough to try a technique, but it might also make him back up or even shoot.

Whatever you do, keep it simple and economical. Maximize your evasive speed by pushing his gun in one direction while you move your body in the opposite direction. Use the principals and techniques advised in the chapter on defensive tactics. There are a variety of techniques that you can use, but whatever tactics you choose, make sure you practice them over and over. A person with little martial arts ability should stick to the basics. Always assume that the attacker will be bigger, stronger, and faster than you, and if what you try turns into a struggle for the weapon, immediately try something else. This is critical when the criminal has a gun because once you start a disarming attempt, you don't want to stop and give him back control of his gun. At that point he will be very scared or angry, and the situation will be even more dangerous for you.

When you are defending yourself against an attacker with a gun, there is a great chance that the gun will fire at least once. It is critical, therefore, that you always keep the muzzle of the gun pointed away from you. If the gun goes off, even if you don't get shot, you may still be burned by the flash, cut by the slide, deafened by the noise, or temporarily blinded if a hot case is ejected into your eye.

If you are going to try to disarm an attacker, you will want to consider where you are as you analyze the threat. If you are in a crowded area and the gun goes off, the bullet may hit an innocent bystander. If you are in an enclosed area like an elevator or hallway and the weapon is a large-caliber handgun, the gunshot may cause you or your principal permanent hearing loss. In the first case you don't want to be responsible for the death of an innocent bystander. In the second case being deaf is better than being dead. You will have to take into consideration all the factors in the situation, including an analysis of your own skills and how immediate the threat is to your own and your principal's life.

Don't plan on taking the gun from the attacker and using it on him. This may or may not become an option. The gun may become disabled in the struggle, especially if it is a semiautomatic. It may also have safeties that you aren't familiar with; if so, it won't shoot. Or it may not be loaded.

If you decide to use a defensive technique instead of escape, negotiation, or another technique to defend your principal or yourself, you have to make the first move. If the attacker moves first, it is too late. Take advantage of making him have to react to your technique. Reaction is always slower than action. There is a way to make his reaction a microsecond slower. Just before you make your move, ask him a question. It can be anything: "Why are you doing this?" or "Do I know you?" This will make him pause for a second while he considers answering you or wonders why you are asking this.

Disarming techniques are only for a situation where you feel that you will be killed if you do nothing. Depending on your expertise level and that of the attacker, the techniques may not work in every situation.

KEEPING CONTROL OF YOUR GUN

Disarming techniques are all designed to take a gun from an attacker who is threatening your life. There are also ways to prevent a gun being taken from you when you are holding it or when you are wearing it concealed.

Defending the Gun in Your Hand

If you are holding someone at gunpoint, the most important element in preventing someone from taking your gun is to keep a distance between yourself and the attacker. If he can't reach you, he can't disarm you. If the attacker tries to move toward you, warn him to stay where he is, slide-step back or to the side to move away from him, or, if you believe that his movement is the start of an immediate attack against your life or the life of your principal, shoot.

If you must hold someone at gunpoint, tell him to put his arms straight up into the air, hands as high as they will go, hands open. Tell the person to slowly turn around so his back is facing you. If there is room, move quietly back and a bit to one side so you won't be where he last saw you if he suddenly turns and attacks. If there is room, make him lie down since it will be more difficult for him to attack you. After he has turned his back to you, tell him to slowly kneel; cross his ankles; using one hand, slowly, lie on his stomach; put his arms straight out to the side; and turn his palms up. Don't let him talk to you or anyone else. If he starts to talk, command him to be quiet. Wait for the police to arrive.

While you are holding someone at gunpoint, relax. Bend your elbows and bring your upper arms against your body to relax your arms. Relax your shoulders and back. You will be able to react much more quickly if you are relaxed than if your muscles are tense. Don't forget about your principal and what is going on while you are occupied.

Protecting Your Holstered Gun

Protection of your holstered gun starts with always making sure it is completely concealed. This requires getting the best holster possible, wearing it on the right place on your body (which will be different for everyone, depending on your body size and shape), wearing the right clothing, and moving in the right way.

Your holster should lie as flat as possible against your body. Leather holsters tend to be better than nylon ones for this. The holster should also cover as much of the gun as possible, especially the trigger guard for safety.

Your clothing must cover your holster and all related equipment. It should be loose enough so it doesn't press against the holstered gun and make a bulge the shape of your gun. It shouldn't be so loose that if you move, your clothes ride up, then get caught on the gun butt and drape over, showing the gun. If you wear an ankle holster, you will need pant legs wide enough and long enough to cover the gun when you walk, step out of a car, go up stairs, or the like. Don't carry heavy objects, such as a gun or extra ammunition in a magazine or speed loader, in your pockets. This will cause your jacket to hang unevenly and show a trained eye that you are carrying such objects. Wear a sturdy belt and cinch it tightly if you wear a holster on your belt. If you don't, your belt will droop to the side of your holster.

Analyze your movements to see how they move your clothing away from, or print the shape of, your holstered gun. If you wear a holster on your right side, if you reach up with your right hand, your jacket will rise, showing the gun muzzle. But if you reach up with your left hand, the right side of your jacket will remain down, concealing your gun. If you wear your holster on the back of your belt, if you bend over at the waist, either your jacket will slide over the gun or the gun will poke up, making a "tent" of your jacket. If you bend at the knees, keeping your back straight, you will maintain concealment of your gun. If you wear your gun on your belt at or toward your side, if your jacket swings open as you reach or gesture, your gun may show. Wear your gun more toward your back or avoid movements that allow your jacket to swing open. You will find many other movements that will tend to show your holstered gun. Analyze each and change your holster position, clothing, or movements to maintain concealment.

Someone has to be very close to you to take your holstered gun. In most cases you can prevent this by being alert, but sometimes in a crowd situation it is more difficult. If you feel someone put his hand on your gun, put your hand on top of his hand, holding it and the gun down, turn quickly toward his elbow, and take control of his elbow, pushing him away.

BODY ARMOR

If you believe that your principal is in danger of being attacked, you might consider soft body armor for your principal and those immediately protecting him or her. The type of soft body armor you choose will depend on the type of attack you expect. There are a number of styles and designs of soft body armor, but these generally will only provide protection against handgun bullets, and each is rated for certain calibers of handguns. Soft body armor won't protect against rifle bullets, knife attacks, or bombs. It also doesn't protect anything but the chest and back areas, so it won't protect against a sniper making a head shot.

If you decide that soft body armor should be worn by your principal, make sure you fully discuss this with him or her to ensure that your principal agrees with the decision. The principal may object to wearing body armor if the weather is very hot or if he or she has to wear it for a long time. Choose a style that is comfortable and gives the most protection. Your principal will have to get clothing that will go over the body armor without making him or her look too bulky.

18

Real-Life Stories

LIFE AS AN EXECUTIVE PROTECTION PROFESSIONAL

Being an EPP has its good points and bad points. Perhaps sharing some personal experiences of an "average" day as an EPP might help those of you just considering this field to make a more educated decision. I (Philip Holder) am going to omit much of what might be considered the juicier details or more dramatic encounters. I will also leave out names and perhaps change some of the locations to protect privacy. Confidentiality is important. Even after one leaves the employ of a principal, all information acquired must still be held in the strictest confidence. For personal and liability reasons, and to protect my own privacy, much must and will always be held in confidence. There are, however, some events that I can relay to you without violating any confidences. I hope that they shed some light on things that might be encountered on the job.

As an EPP I was very fortunate in many ways. My principals always treated me with respect and as a valued member of the family. With most of them, when they went to a restaurant, I ate with them (and on their tab). I had access to their clubs, vehicles, and pools and was treated well at holidays, my birthday, and similar occasions. This is not always the case.

I have heard many horror stories from fellow EPPs. Some say that they were treated as a necessary nuisance. Often (more so in corporate work) an EPP gets little respect for his or her efforts. I have heard of EPPs working 70 or more hours a week, virtually giving up any personal life, and then being given the boot with little or no notice because of changes within the company that employed them. This can happen, so take note: When you are marketing yourself as an EPP, make the interview a two-way street. While your prospective principal is evaluating you, you should be evaluating your prospective principal (and his or her company). If you are able, casually talk to other employees or detail members to get a feel for how they feel they are treated.

THE UP SIDE

Having an appreciative principal can be a real plus. I remember one instance when it was important that some sensitive information be personally taken to the West Coast and a confidential response brought back (I was on the East Coast). My principal felt that I should be the courier. I flew out first-class and was provided with a wonderful room on one of the executive-suite floors. I had access to the health clubs and masseuses and was comped to the finest restaurants in town. I was allowed to go out a few days early for some rest and relaxation, and my principal's company picked up the tab. My principal did not go, so the trip had little responsibility other than an exchange of information. As a very trusted employee, I was selected for the job.

THE DOWN SIDE

Not everything is a bed of roses, even with the best of principals. I remember being woken from a sound sleep at 2:30 A.M. by the ringing of my telephone. "Hello," I mumbled, half asleep. "We have to go to the city. We're on our way to pick you up. Be ready in about twenty minutes," said my principal. With no further comment I heard the phone disconnect. I got up and threw on my clothes and splashed some cold water in my face. Almost exactly in twenty minutes my principal's vehicle pulled up in front of my house, and I dashed out and jumped in the car. It was cold and damp out. I would much rather have been in my nice warm bed, but this was my job and my responsibility.

My principal and two other employees were in the car. He informed me that a family member working within his company had apparently been poisoned. He wasn't sure about the details. The injured party was in the hospital in a major city about three hours away. He was having his stomach pumped. My principal strongly suspected that the poisoning was intentional, but he was not certain. I was elected to escort the target to safety.

It was about 6:00 A.M. when we pulled into the city. Working girls were still on the street corners and approached the car at every intersection. We located the hospital in a rather sleazy section of town. My principal wanted to go in alone. I designated one man to stay with the car and the other to watch the lobby, and I remained stationed at the door through which we planned to exit. I watched carefully for anything unusual until my principal approached with the intended target. He (the target) looked like he had been beaten with an ugly stick. I motioned for the car and we all converged curbside and got into the car without hesitation. I thought to myself, "Good, we're out of here," but no such luck. The target indicated that he needed to go back to his hotel room to pick up personal belongings and a large amount of cash held in the hotel safe.

When we reached the hotel, I had the driver drop me off curbside. I went ahead to advance the hotel and the target's room. I wasn't sure what I would find because the hotel room was where the suspected poisoning had taken place. I knew very well that if it was in fact an intentional poisoning, the perpetrator might still be on the premises to find something or to finish the job. I entered the room carefully and completed my search. I signaled the driver to prepare to drop the target. I met the target curbside and escorted him to his room. I had instructed the driver of our vehicle to keep the car moving until I signaled him to come pick us up. Quickly, the target threw his belongings into his suitcase while I stood watch. We then proceeded to the main desk, where he claimed his things from the hotel safe. I signaled the car for a pickup, and we rendezvoused curbside. Within seconds we were on our way.

We had already planned, on our way to the city, which location would be best for the safe haven, so we plotted a course for home. I instructed the driver to zigzag an indirect route down many different roads and to use all possible measures to assure that we were not followed to the safe haven. As I remember, it was about 11:30 A.M. when we arrived at the safe haven. We settled the target in, and then I escorted my principal home. I was then ready to have the driver drop me at home.

WHAT ABOUT YOU?

Does this sound exciting to you? It was not! It was a long and tiring night, but that often goes with the territory. To be an EPP, you have to be willing to take the poop with the gravy. It is not a job that you can do when it is convenient. It is a job that you do when you are needed. Sometimes you will be able to plan and therefore create a reasonable degree of security. Other times you may encounter something like the incident I have described here where there is no time to plan and where you are flying by the seat of your pants. In either event, you are the one responsible for the life and safety of others. You must be prepared.

19

Things to Consider When Choosing Executive Protection as a Career

When someone tells me (Philip Holder) his or her true motivation for wanting to become an EPP, I can pretty much predict what caliber of EPP that person will be from that information alone. Your motivation will have great bearing on your job performance. If someone indicates to me that he is a tough guy and that being an EPP is a way that he can utilize his prowess to make money, I know that he is not going to be in line for the EPP of the Year award. Likewise, if he views himself as a sort of "Dirty Harry" figure who will get the bad guys, I am certain of his early (probably involuntary) retirement.

If you feel the need to provide a valuable, quality service, you may be EPP material. If you take pride in helping others to feel more safe and secure, you may be EPP material. If you are humbled by the prospect of having another person entrust his or her life into your hands, you may be EPP material. If your work ethic leads you to realize the importance of doing the best possible job simply because you expect the best from yourself, you may be EPP material.

At first glance, many people think that being an EPP sounds like a glamorous career. In fact, becoming an EPP requires great personal sacrifice. My personal feeling is that it is better suited to the single unattached person; however, I am sure that there are those who would disagree with me.

Being an EPP often means that your family time can be severely limited. It is also more difficult to make vacation plans and other personal plans. You may be on the road a lot. Sometimes, depending on the people, this can have a negative impact on a marriage and on your family life. If you have a spouse and/or children, you may want to accept only lower-risk assignments. If you are maimed or killed, who will provide both financial and emotional support for your family? As well, is your family emotionally and financially equipped to care for you if you are temporarily or permanently disabled? I would suggest that for the family person, going into or staying in this profession should be a family decision. Be certain that everyone is comfortable with this choice, or someone involved will end up feeling cheated.

When you are making your career choice, weigh in the lifestyle that you visualize for yourself both now and in the years to come. Do this before choosing the field of executive protection. You will do yourself, your family, and any future principal(s) a gross injustice if you have not examined your choice carefully. No matter how much money you make, or what perks are included, if you do not enjoy both your work and your life outside of your work, the pay will mean little.

20

Pay and Benefits

You can make a very comfortable living as an EPP, but it is doubtful that you will ever be featured on "Lifestyles of the Rich and Famous." It is best that you become an EPP because you feel a sense of purpose and accomplishment in providing a service, rather than having the expectation of becoming filthy rich. As well, because you need to maintain a low profile, it would be inappropriate to seek headlines as an active operative. Before you ask, "What will I make?" you must first ask yourself if this is really the line of work that you want to be in.

Pay scales can vary dramatically depending on a number of factors. Some basic guidelines are appropriate when spelling out your salary requirements to a potential employer. Much will depend on the following criteria:

1. Will you be working as a single agent or on a detail?
2. Do you have fairly regular hours, or are you on call 24 hours a day, 7 days a week?
3. Are you a full-time regular employee, or are you on call as an independent contractor?
4. What benefits, if any, are included as part of your employment package?
5. What is the risk factor?

These criteria will all affect the compensation that you should expect.

Generally speaking, you will be paid more as a single agent because you are accepting greater responsibility. As a single agent, you must wear many hats. Although this does not hold true in all circumstances, more often than not, expect higher compensation as a single agent. However, many corporate security heads pay their agents quite well. Too, it is possible that you may be offered a position by someone who is not extremely wealthy but who feels the need for an EPP. This might be an exception to the rule of making more as a single EPP.

Some positions require that you be on call 7 days a week, 24 hours a day. This does not mean that you will work all of these hours. Some weeks you may work 80 hours. Other weeks you may work 5 hours. The point is that you can be called at any time. You might receive a phone call at three in the morning telling you to pack and leave for a distant location immediately. If you are on call, you must go. When you are on call, expect that your life is not your own. You will carry a cell phone, a beeper, and a radio wherever you go. Don't plan on staying at the amusement park with your kids if the beeper sounds or the cell phone rings. When you are called, you go. This lifestyle is certainly deserving of higher salary considerations.

With other positions, you may be given fairly specific hours. This is more likely when you are working as part of a detail. If having more personal time is important to you, you may be willing to take a little less cash in return for a more stable schedule. Be forewarned, though, that there is really no such thing as a fixed schedule when you are an EPP. Getting regular hours is more the exception than the rule anywhere in this business.

Another factor is your employment status. Will you work as a direct employee or as an independent contractor? There are benefits and drawbacks to each.

As an employee, you often have greater protection against personal lawsuits as long as you stay within the job description and responsibilities as outlined in your employment contract. You will want to consult a lawyer about this when you are negotiating your contract for employment. As well, as an employee you may be covered by your employers insurance(s). You may be able to participate in retirement and group health insurance plans, and your employer will deduct your taxes, Social Security, and other withholdings, making your tax return a bit simpler. The downside is that your employer can exercise greater control over you.

As an independent contractor, you have the greater responsibility of providing your own health insurance, filing quarterly tax returns and payments, and so on. You may find that you can ask for more money because your employer will be saving on many hidden costs of retaining an employee. You may want to check with your accountant to see if working as an independent contractor may provide you with certain tax advantages. Every case is different. In any event, have an employment contract. Have the contract drawn up or reviewed by a competent attorney. In the event of a dispute, it will make problems easier to resolve. It may even save a strained relationship between employer and EPP by providing clarity and protection for both parties.

Many principals do not want to hire independents because they like having the extra flexibility that comes with having control of a direct employee. Remember that as an independent contractor, you may retain the right to refuse an assignment that you are uncomfortable with. This is all negotiable. You must decide what works best for you and what you are most at ease with. You can then adjust your salary requirements accordingly.

Another thing to consider is the benefit package. Will you have a retirement plan? Will you get a company car? Will you have paid vacation time? Is there a health club or country club membership attached? One valuable perk is company-paid health insurance. This can add a considerable value to the employment package. These are all things that must be considered when addressing your salary requirements.

Last but not least, what is the risk factor? If the risk is low, you can probably expect to make less. If the risk is high, ask for a salary that is commensurate with the risk. Remember, you can only die once, and then you are out of the equation. Find out as much as possible about your prospective principal's level of risk before submitting a salary request. Find out if there have been any previous attacks on him or her. Find out what the nature of the attacks were. Find out what types of enemies the prospective principal may have. Evaluate his or her type of business and the risks that may be inherent to it. A sports figure may have a much lower chance of attack with lethal intent than someone who runs an abortion clinic or who conducts experiments on animals. Know the turf before you accept an agreement.

As general parameters, I would think the following to be reasonable in today's market. You, however must decide what you think your time and talents are worth. These are just broad estimations. If you are working with a detail and/or as a direct employee, you might consider a starting range between $35,000 and $50,000, depending on the benefits involved, the hours, and the other factors discussed in this chapter. As the benefit package increases, you can move the cash compensation accordingly. Again, these are rough estimates, and if you are an experienced EPP, you may be able to ask for (and receive) more. With great perks and regular hours, you may choose to accept a lower figure, especially if this is your first assignment. If the assignments have an exceptionally high risk factor, the sky is the limit. Find out what the market will bear and then ask yourself if it is worth it to you. Ultimately, the decision is totally yours.

As an independent part-time or "as-needed" EPP, you must again weigh the risk and the other factors discussed in this chapter. Depending on risk and responsibilities and the duration of the assignment, compensation can vary drastically. As they say, things are cheaper by the dozen. You can expect to make more per day or hour with a one-day assignment than you will for a two-week assignment. A range of $300 to $1,500 per day can be used as a rough barometer. This again depends on your experience, the risk factor, and so on. You may need to go lower or higher, depending on all of these factors. As an independent working on an "as-needed" basis, you will, in all likelihood, not have to concern yourself with benefits because there will normally be none.

21

How to Avoid Getting Fired

In this book we give you valuable information on what to do as a professional in the field of executive protection. Now let us discuss some of the things that will get you fired. Many Americans go to a foreign country and, because of lack of knowledge of that culture, offend people whom they encounter purely out of ignorance. An EPP who doesn't know the turf can encounter similar pitfalls. There are certain things that you must be aware "not to do" or you will end up either demoted or fired.

METHODS BY WHICH TO GET FIRED

1. Become personally involved with your principal's family, friends, or associates.
2. Get caught in bed with a member of your principal's family or a family friend (you know, like all the secret agents do in the movies).
3. Use your position for personal gain (either professional, personal, or social).
4. Try to use your principal's name to gain personal leverage.
5. Talk openly about your work to others (word has a way of getting around).
6. Live night and day for your work with no rest and relaxation (R and R).

Any of the actions listed here will ultimately result in your demise as an EPP. If you would like to get fired and drummed out of the corps, these are ways to do it.

PERSONAL DETACHMENT

Do not get personally involved with your principal, his or her family, or friends. Keep your social and personal life separate from theirs. No matter how cordial things seem at first, you can't mix business with pleasure in this field. It will cause both you and your principal to view each other in less than professional terms. A problem in the friendship will directly affect your position and effectiveness as an EPP. Remember too that your principal, as your employer, wields the greater power. If a personal problem does arise, you will end up with the short end of the stick.

In the same manner that you should keep your relationship with your principal on a professional level, you should maintain a professional relationship with his or her friends, family, and associates. Any camaraderie between you and these individuals constitutes a direct conflict of interest. You leave yourself open to suspicion and doubt on many levels. Your position becomes precarious at best. Let's say that through no fault of your own, personal information about your principal's life leaks out to a friend or associate of your principal. Even if you are not the person who is guilty of passing the information on, you will be suspect. As well, a mutual friend to both you and your principal may put you in an uncomfortable position by attempting to make you take sides if he or she has a disagreement with your principal. This may even occur behind the scenes without your knowledge. The person may say to your principal, "Well, I'm not the only person who thinks you're wrong, so does [your name]." This is not going to make you look good, even if it is not true. You must be above reproach in your principal's eyes. He or she must know that you are discreet and dependable and that you can keep your mouth shut. Stay away from your principal's family. You are not a family friend; you are a professional protector hired to provide security.

INDISCRETION

Because of the closeness with which you may often work, personal temptations may arise. If they are not on your part, they may be, for example, on the part of your principal's pretty young daughter (or son, for female EPPs). Avoid these situations like the plague. Make no advances toward people connected to your principal, even if you are encouraged to do so. As well, politely laugh off any advances from those close to your principal. You must politely discourage such relationships without causing the other party to lose face. As important as it is to keep this personal detachment, you do not want to make an enemy of someone close to your principal in the process.

PERSONAL GAIN

Some people in this field let their egos get the best of them. This is the kiss of death. Do not use your position for personal gain, or you will not last long in this business. Don't brag or use your position (or your principal's name) to impress women (or men). You are not James Bond. This is not the movies, and you are not a "double-naught spy." You are a professional protective agent, so behave like one at all times. If you are flirtatious with members of the opposite sex at a cocktail party, for instance, you will be perceived as lacking the necessary focus to do your job effectively. You will also be demonstrating your lack of professionalism and character. Do your carousing on your own time. When you are on duty, your time belongs to your employer. If you are attempting to be "upwardly mobile" by soliciting other work while in the employ of your principal, you are inviting a pink slip. If you are good at your job, new opportunities will come your way without your making a fool of yourself by networking on your principal's time.

LEVERAGE

If you try to get the best theater tickets or the best table at your principal's favorite restaurant by dropping his or her name, you will soon get a reputation as a blowhard.

You can depend that the restaurant staff will casually let your principal know about your lame attempt to gain power through him or her at the first possible opportunity. Can you blame them? How would you view someone using that tactic on you? In short, don't flaunt your position for personal gain. You have already agreed on what your compensation for your services will be when you negotiated your contract. Don't attempt to squeeze more out of the deal.

LOOSE LIPS

Some people love to come home and talk about their day at the office. Others talk about their day over a beer with the guys. As an EPP, you should talk to no one about your job, your principal, your coworkers, or your principal's family, friends, or associates. This includes your best friend, your husband or wife, or any significant other. This does not just hold true during your employment. It holds true for all time. It doesn't matter whether you liked or disliked your principal, or under what circumstances you left his or her employ. Any information you obtained, both professional and personal, should remain confidential for all time. This is a question of character. It has nothing to do with your principal. It has everything to do with your character and integrity. This will have a major impact on how you are viewed by others as well.

BURNOUT

There are many ways to avoid burnout. Meditation, physical exercise, and recreational activities are probably the most common. In addition to these, we have another suggestion: Don't live for your job. A good EPP takes time for family, friends, and recreation. This will help to keep you balanced and reduce your stress levels (and being an EPP can be stressful). If you immerse yourself totally into your work 24 hours a day, 7 days a week, it will not show that you are a dedicated EPP, it will show that you are a "nut." You will soon burn out. Your job performance will suffer, and you will ultimately find yourself fired or, if they want to be kinder in letting you go, you will become a victim of downsizing.

To be an EPP, you must be calm and have the ability to make important decisions under pressure and frequently within limited time constraints. You must always have a clear perception of what is occurring or what could occur. You must be aware of how others around you think and behave. This will not happen if you live in a vacuum. If you perceive life from a limited vantage point, you will be unaware of much that may happen right before your eyes. In short, a good EPP is a well-rounded person. Get out once in a while!

If you become a victim of burnout, you will be of no value to yourself or others. Negotiate with your principal times for your vacation and R and R that don't conflict with his or her schedule. Get plenty of rest and plenty of exercise. Make sure that you are eating properly. These habits will all improve your health and reduce stress. A diet of caffeine and sugary donuts will help to give you a short fuse and turn you into a human vibrator. If you are healthy and alert, you will be happier, and so will your principal. He or she will have a more alert and aware protector and therefore feel more secure and comfortable. After all, your job is to provide for the safety and comfort of your principal. This is another way in which you can accomplish this.

If you are working for a corporate executive, you may have access to a health club. Many companies have them on-site for employees. If not, get a good piece of home equipment such as a strength training machine. Consult an exercise professional to find out which is best for you. If you are on the road a lot, develop a daily program of calisthenics that you do when you wake up or before going to bed. Structure a set time (as much as possible) and keep a routine, or you will soon neglect doing your exercises.

Watch your diet. If you are flying, avoid salty foods and drink plenty of liquids. Stay away from alcohol (of course) or anything else that will dry you out. The air in an aircraft cabin is usually very dry. Doing this will help reduce fatigue and jet lag. If you will be spending a great deal of time sedentary (riding in a car, sitting in an office, or the like), eat plenty of fresh fruits and vegetables and grains. This will help avoid digestive disorders like constipation. Also, pasta is rich in complex carbohydrates, a great source of energy. Whenever possible, don't skip meals. Your performance at three or four in the afternoon will be directly affected by what you had (or didn't have) for breakfast.

I (Philip Holder) have found that the most time-effective way to maximize my stress-reduction efforts is through meditation. I feel that I get the most effect per minute invested using this method. Often, when I have a spare couple of minutes, I find a quiet place to meditate. In just minutes I come away feeling relaxed and renewed.

There are a variety of meditation methods available. All involve relaxation techniques. Some use breathing exercises. Some utilize visualization and imagery. Some incorporate a combination of these techniques. Meditation, like everything else, is a skill that is developed through both instruction by a competent teacher and diligent practice on your part. You can find instructors of meditation through various martial arts organizations, through yoga organizations, through holistic health organizations, or simply by looking up meditation in the phone directory or on the World Wide Web. The Web is a great tool to find resources if you have access to an online computer and have good Web browser software. The best way to find competent instruction is through referral. As well, do your homework first. Learn a little about the various methods of meditation so that you can make an educated decision about which one will best suit you. When you are armed with knowledge, seek out a quality instructor.

Conclusion

Being an EPP can be a rewarding career. It can also be disastrous for those who are ill prepared and for their principal(s). This book was written for three purposes, all of equal importance. First, it was written to provide those considering a career as an EPP valuable information that might be helpful in making an educated decision about entering this field. Second, it was written to provide a continuing source of educational information for those actively pursuing a career in executive protection. Third, it was written to help those who are seeking to find a qualified EPP with information that will help them in hiring the right person. Becoming an EPP, developing your skills as an active EPP, or enlisting the services of an EPP are all serious matters that must be approached from a position of knowledge. We hope that this book will provide that service.

The authors welcome your comments. They may be contacted in the following ways:

Web page: http://home.sprynet.com/sprynet/masters

E-mail: masters@sprynet.com

Phone: (215) 295-8062

Fax: (215) 295-8063

Master's Realm Inc.

128 Independence Drive

Morrisville, PA 19067

Appendix

Sample Checklists

This appendix provides some sample checklists that you can use for organizing the protection of your principal. You should make a checklist for every aspect of your day, trip, or event. Keep all of your checklists current. Make changes as your detail members change, persons are added to or removed from your principal's party, locations change, and you go to new facilities. Add anything you think is important to these checklists. Don't assume that you will remember any details of the trip. No one can remember every little detail, and you have far more important things to have your mind on. Use these checklists as a guide for developing your own checklists and add to them as your experience develops.

ROUTE-PLAN SURVEY

Primary routes (number of lanes, intersections, one-way streets, and other traffic features)

Alternate routes

Safe haven(s)

Medical facilities

Checked vulnerable areas

    Access roads

    Bridges

    Highway ramps

    Intersections

    Traffic lights

    Location(s)

    Length of time to travel

    Anticipated causes for delay

    Synchronized lights (Y/N)

    Railroad tracks

    Congested areas

    Hills and other inclines

Overpasses

Buildings overlooking route(s)

Sewers and storm drains

Choke points

Location of law-enforcement departments

Checkpoints

ADVANCE CHECKLIST

1. Location/address
2. Telephone #(s)
3. Escort
     Telephone 1
     Telephone 2
4. Fire dept.
     Telephone
     Distance
     Response time
5. Police dept.
     Telephone
     Distance
     Response time
6. Ambulance co.
     Telephone
     Distance
     Response time
7. Doctor
     Telephone
     Distance
     Response time
8. Pharmacy
     Telephone
     Distance
     Response time
9. Hospital
     Telephone
     Distance
     Response time
10. Arrival and departure areas
11. Parking area
12. Host name and information
13. Entrances and exits to function room
14. Function room(s)

15. Elevators
    Operators
    Capacity
    Weight capacity
    Date of last inspection
16. Evacuation route(s)
17. Nearest restrooms
18. Nearest telephone
19. Nearest privacy room
20. Physical inspection of any room in which the principal will be
21. Checkpoints
22. Background checks of anyone who will be near to the principal
23. Type of function(s)
24. Total expected time of visit
25. Seating charts
26. Will gifts or packages be exchanged?
27. Head table
28. Receiving line
29. Press coverage
    Type
    Agencies
    Number of reporters
30. Hotel management/support
    Room-service manager
        Telephone
    Restaurant manager
        Telephone
    Parking attendant
        Telephone
    Other
        Telephone
    Other
        Telephone
    Other
        Telephone
    Other
        Telephone
    Room assignments
    Name and room # of each person in party
31. Extra room keys to
32. Guest roster of neighbors (Who is staying alongside, above, and below the principal?)
33. Search/technical sweep
    Time
    Date
    Results

INDIVIDUAL BIOGRAPHICAL OUTLINE

1. Name:
2. Physical description:
3. Home address:
4. Home phone:
5. Business address:
6. Business phone(s):
7. Neighbors' address(es):
8. Neighbors' phone(s):
9. School information for dependents:
10. Medical information:
11. ID information (photos, fingerprints, handwriting samples, voice recordings, etc.):
12. Known enemies and/or antagonists:
13. Licenses, registrations, permits:
14. Regular activities and interests:
15. Favorite clothing:
16. Professional numbers (doctor, lawyer, accountant, insurance):
17. Financial institutions (banks, etc.):

SAFE HAVEN CHECKLIST

List the nearest of the following:

1. Police locations
2. Other security locations
3. Fire stations
4. Hospitals
5. Shopping centers
6. Nearby large companies or factories
7. Foreign or U.S. government facilities
8. Military facilities and offices
9. Any nearby facility that includes security details

ADVANCE EPP CHECKLIST

1. Date assigned
2. Location
3. Event date(s)
4. Date briefed
    Information "on" the record:
    Information "off" the record:
5. Duration of assignment

6. Hotels, etc. (where applicable)
7. Number of detail members
8. Detail leader
9. Advance leader
10. Advance team members
11. State police
12. Local police
13. FBI
14. Other
15. Transportation (plane, helicopter, auto, rail, other)
16. Other security measures (electronic surveillance, etc.)
17. Arrival point
18. Arrival time
19. Departure point
20. Departure time

BAGGAGE CONTROL SHEET

Color _____   Assigned to _____   Room # _____

Baggage responsibility/accountability

Location _____   Date _____

Number _____Date/Time
Baggage count 1.
Baggage count 2.
Baggage count 3.

Members of Baggage Detail
Driver _____
Supervisor _____
Others _____

Comments:

VEHICLE SEATING CHART

Vehicle 1

1. (Driver)
2.
3.

4.
5.
6.
7.

Vehicle 2

1.   (Driver)
2.
3.
4.
5.
6.
7.

Vehicle 3

1.   (Driver)
2.
3.
4.
5.
6.
7.

Vehicle 4

1.   (Driver)
2.
3.
4.
5.
6.
7.

Vehicle 5

1.   (Driver)
2.
3.
4.

5.
6.
7.

AIRCRAFT SEATING CHART

General Information

1. Departure
2. Destination
3. Date
4. Type of aircraft

Crew

1. Pilot
2. Copilot
3. Navigator
4. Crew chief
5. Crew members

Seating

Name _____ Seat # _____ Aisle/Center(s)/Window _____

Index

Related Butterworth-Heinemann Titles

Security Consulting
Charles A. Sennewald
1995   192pp   0-7506-9643-5   pb $34.95

Guard Force Management
Lucien Canton
1995   144pp   0-7506-9299-5   hc $34.95

Securing Home and Business
A Guide to the Electronic Security Industry
Simon Hakim ◆ Erwin A. Blackstone
1996   208pp   0-7506-9629-X   hc $44.95

Legal Guidelines for the Use of Force
in the Private Sector
John Dale Hartman
1997   268pp   0-7506-9562-5   hc $44.95

Feel free to visit our web site at: http://www.bh.com

These books are available from all good bookstores or in case of difficulty call: 1-800-366-2665 in the U.S. or +44-1865-310366 in Europe.

E-Mail Mailing List

An e-mail mailing list giving information on latest releases, special promotions/ offers and other news relating to Butterworth-Heinemann business titles is available. To subscribe, send an e-mail message to majordomo@world.std.com. Include in message body (not in subject line) subscribe bh-business